THE DRAGON AWAKES

THE DRAGON AWAKES

THE REBIRTH OF A RUGBY NATION

ANDREW WILLIAMS

MAINSTREAM
PUBLISHING
EDINBURGH AND LONDON

Copyright © Andrew Williams, 2000
All rights reserved
The moral right of the author has been asserted

First published in Great Britain in 2000 by
MAINSTREAM PUBLISHING COMPANY (EDINBURGH) LTD
7 Albany Street
Edinburgh EH1 3UG

ISBN 1 84018 328 4

No part of this book may be reproduced or transmitted in any form or by any means without written permission from the publisher, except by a reviewer who wishes to quote brief passages in connection with a review written for insertion in a newspaper, magazine or broadcast

A catalogue record for this book is available from the British Library

Typeset in Impact and Janson
Printed and bound in Great Britain by
Butler and Tanner Ltd, Frome and London

To my sons, Rhys and Haydn Williams

CONTENTS

Acknowledgements   9
Introduction: The Golden Era, or a Golden Albatross?   11

1	Enter The Redeemer	21
2	The Five Nations	45
3	Putting The Roof On	61
4	The Build-up Begins	69
5	Some Time In The Sun	85
6	The Rugby World Cup	95
7	Intermission	121
8	The Six Nations	125
9	The Gloves Are Off	137
10	The Way Forward	155

Statistics: Wales Under Graham Henry   169

ACKNOWLEDGEMENTS

This book grew out of a conversation in the pub with Neville Depree. Neville, another Kiwi transplanted to Wales, supplied the photographs for the book, and I would like to acknowledge all the help he gave me along the way. I would also like to thank Rose for her support. Sharing a house with three rugby fanatics cannot be easy, yet somehow she manages to preserve her, and our, sanity. I owe a great debt of thanks to Bill Campbell, Caroline Budge and the long-suffering staff at Mainstream Publishing. I am indebted to the management and playing members of the Welsh squad, who were all extremely helpful throughout the project. Particular thanks to David Pickering and Steve Black, who not only gave of their time, but also went out of their way to make me welcome in the squad. Finally, a huge thank you to Graham Henry, who took time out of an incredibly busy schedule to help make this book work.

INTRODUCTION

THE GOLDEN ERA, OR A GOLDEN ALBATROSS?

IT WAS A PERFECT AUTUMN DAY IN NOVEMBER 1974. I was playing rugby for London Welsh. The two pitches at Old Deer Park were in use, as the first and second fifteens were both playing at home. When I walked through the gates of Old Deer Park at 1 p.m. there were already hundreds of spectators milling around. In the clubhouse, the bar was doing a brisk trade and by 2.30 there was a crowd of several thousand, the majority of which was clustered around the second team pitch. Throughout the early '70s, the Richmond-based club was the meeting place for the many Welsh exiles living in London and large crowds were the norm, but usually they would be packing the stand in the shadow of the Kew Gardens pagoda. Today the focus of attention had shifted and the crowd were lined along the touchlines of the practice pitch.

The cause of all this attention, directed at the humble second-string outfit, was the presence in their midst of one of the legends of Welsh rugby. J.P.R. Williams had toured South Africa with the hugely successful British Lions team. After the tour he had stayed on for an extended vacation, but had returned in mid-November and was using this match to prove his fitness prior to playing for Wales against the All Blacks.

THE DRAGON AWAKES

These were heady times at the Richmond-based club. Many of the household names of Welsh rugby turned out for us and the club boasted that it was the best in the world. London Welsh embodied all that was best in Welsh rugby and in those days we had much to be proud of, at both club and international level. Welsh rugby was riding high. The national team was seen as being one of the strongest in the world, on a par with the mighty All Blacks. Wales had provided the backbone of the Lions teams, which had been so successful in New Zealand in 1971, and again in South Africa in 1974. Max Boyce's outside-half factory was working overtime, and it was a joy to be a Welsh rugby supporter. As well as being an extremely effective outfit, Wales played attractive, exhilarating rugby and it seemed to all of us back then that this was the natural state of affairs. Nobody believed that the golden era could ever end. Little did we realise that the glorious teams of the '70s were to hang like an albatross around the neck of Welsh rugby for the next twenty-five years.

The golden opportunity to build on the successes of the '70s was passed up and over the course of the next quarter of a century, through a mixture of bad luck and bad management, we went from being the kings of rugby to the clowns of the game. Coaches came and went, great players struggled in mediocre teams before going north to rugby league and record defeat piled on record defeat. Occasional flashes of brilliance were invariably hailed as the dawning of a new golden age, only for the dream to be shattered as the Welsh team reverted to the losing ways which had by now become habitual.

A number of factors conspired to keep Welsh rugby well and truly on the ropes, and a lot of the blame must be laid at the door of the Welsh Rugby Union [WRU]. A perfect illustration of Wales's problems is afforded by a look at the team of 1988. In that year, Wales won the Triple Crown and shared the championship with France. The side contained some great players, most notably Jonathan Davies, Robert Jones, Mark

The Dragon Awakes

Ring, Ieuan Evans and Robert Norster. The catalyst for this winning Welsh team was perceived to be Jonathan Davies, a classic Welsh outside-half; mercurial, infuriatingly unpredictable and arrogantly confident on the field. It seemed that here was a player who might just form the nucleus of a winning Welsh team.

The success of 1988 gave us something to build on and there was hope in the Welsh camp at last. However, having won the Triple Crown, the Welsh team were packed off on a tour to New Zealand. The tour was a disaster. The schedule was too tough – even the New Zealand coach admitted this, and said that he would never have accepted such an itinerary for his team. The travel arrangements were second-rate, as was the accommodation. In both Tests of that tour, Wales conceded over fifty points. The results were seen as an all-time low for the game in Wales. The gulf between the two sides on the pitch was mirrored by the differences between the players off the field. The New Zealand players were, to all intents and purposes, professionals. They were making money through sponsorship and product endorsements. The Welsh players at the time were still strictly amateur. As Jonathan Davies commented afterwards, 'Our players weren't even compensated for time lost at work. It was actually costing them to play for their country, while the All Blacks were making money from their position as national heroes.'

Off the rugby field, Davies was a pragmatic, hardheaded realist. He didn't object to the New Zealand players making money; he just wanted equality for the Welsh players. When the touring party returned home, Davies let it be known that he had prepared a report on the tour, outlining the players' feelings about what had gone on and suggesting that improvements needed to be made to avoid such a disaster being repeated. The WRU snubbed his offer of help and did what comes naturally to them: they sacked the coach. The powers that be continued to pay tribute to the concept of amateurism, while the nations of the Southern Hemisphere circumnavigated the regulations. The fact of the matter was that Wales were a bunch of amateurs playing against professionals, and as long as that system persisted we could never compete. The ostrich-like attitude of the governing body exacerbated the problem. It frustrated the players, who understood the situation and increasingly felt that they were being taken advantage of. 'We are expected to behave like professionals,' said Davies, 'but we are treated like amateurs.'

The general sense of frustration led to a mass exodus from the Welsh team. Less than a year after winning the Triple Crown, Jonathan Davies went north, joining Widnes for a record fee, reported to be £240,000. Half a dozen players from the Welsh squad followed Davies' example and went professional. 'Shamateurism' was a term that was used a great deal at the time, and it really did sum up the team's problems. New Zealanders were being paid for product endorsement, top rugby players in England found lucrative work which left plenty of free time for training, but the same options were not open to Welsh players. Product endorsement would not have been allowed by the WRU, and the Welsh economy simply wasn't structured to provide the kind of nominal careers enjoyed by London-based players. If you were a Welsh rugby player and you wanted to make money, you went north. And they did, in droves. Realistically, few nations could have hoped to compete, given the steady drain to northern clubs. Players of the calibre of Adrian Hadley, Dai Young, Scott Gibbs, Allan Bateman and Scott Quinnell are not easily replaced, and it is probably significant that Welsh fortunes only improved when the movement north was stopped and these players returned to the union game.

The national team and the top Welsh clubs, once revered the world over, had lost the respect of the rugby world. The fiercely competitive Anglo-Welsh matches were a thing of the past. The advent of league rugby had resulted in nationalism, which meant

The Dragon Awakes

that the top clubs in Wales were involved in an insular and parochial league, dominated by a handful of sides. Most of these games were meaningless, one-sided contests. Welsh rugby was stagnating in a mire of insularity.

In 1998 the game in Wales hit an all-time low, with Kevin Bowring as the current holder of the poisoned chalice. A product of the London Welsh club, Bowring was a respected coach who was struggling to encourage the Welsh team to play expansive rugby which might enable them to compete on the world stage. His teams displayed moments of brilliance which gave hope to the faithful, but his days were numbered after we leaked sixty points to England in the Five Nations tournament. The *coup de grâce* was administered, appropriately, by the French.

At this time, the dejected state of Welsh rugby was epitomised by the fact that we didn't even have a home stadium. The old National Stadium had been torn down in order to build a new stadium which most of us didn't think we needed. Welsh rugby was a hotbed of factionalism, infighting and politicking. The nation was divided between those who saw the building of a new stadium as symbolic of a new start, the beginnings of an attempt to re-establish Wales as a leading rugby nation, and those who felt that the building was an irrelevance which ignored the fact that the game was dying on its feet.

Most supporters felt emasculated by the entire affair. Edicts were passed down by the WRU with no apparent concern for them, the grass roots of the game in Wales. We were playing our matches at the home of English soccer, Wembley Stadium. It was a tremendous testimony to the loyalty of the Welsh fans that despite the best attempts of the WRU to alienate its support, they flocked in their thousands to London to watch their team play. These fans travelled in droves to the English capital, but we could never really feel at home in London. Our first 'home' outing of the Home International season of 1998 was at Wembley, against the Scots. It brought victory, but little joy. The

THE DRAGON AWAKES

rugby had been uninspiring, and Wales had simply been the better of two poor sides. The train journey back to Newport after the Scottish game was a sober one – the jollity which usually accompanies Welsh supporters on away journeys was missing. There was merely a depressed silence as the weary fans slept after a victory which most thought had been somewhat fortunate.

When we travelled back up to Wembley for the French match on 5 April 1998, we went more in hope than expectation. That afternoon, the French gave us a lesson in how the modern game should be played. One man, Thomas Castaignède, gave a brilliant demonstration of the team's skills: he ran the ball from suicidal positions and effortlessly cut holes in the Welsh defence. We were shown to be too slow in both thought and deed. The gap between the two sides was so great that I could not even bring myself to feel depressed by the result. It was a spectacular game of running rugby, and you couldn't help but marvel at the skill of the French side. In the bar afterwards I chatted with the French supporters, who were marvellous. 'Never mind,' said one comforting Frenchman, 'next year it may be different.' I just shook my head. Nothing could be done in twelve months that would bring us within sight of the fantastic French side. We were quite simply playing different games. In addition, next year we would have to play them on their own patch, inside the magnificent new Stade de France. Fat chance!

Many cynical fans claimed it was a good job we were hosting the World Cup, because it was only as the host nation that we could be sure to be taking part: if we weren't hosts, we would be facing difficult qualifying matches against the likes of Spain and Portugal.

Of course, by next season we would hopefully have a new stadium. The attitude of most Welsh fans towards the building site that was to become our new home illustrated the general pessimism in the game in Wales. The majority viewed the new

16

stadium as a white elephant, and felt that the money could have been better spent developing the Welsh game, bringing on young players in our schools and clubs. Instead we had spent millions on a new ground which many, in an all-pervasive fit of black, Welsh despondency, believed would not be ready in time for the forthcoming Rugby World Cup. Although we had no ground it didn't matter, many claimed, because we had no team to play there anyway.

Still, I consoled myself with the thought that at least things couldn't get any worse. Wrong again. The International Rugby Board had decreed that in the summer of 1998, Wales should tour South Africa. Our shell-shocked team was going to the lair of the world champions on a tour which none of them wanted. The team that went off to South Africa was psychologically shattered and depleted by injuries.

The tour took place under new management, Dennis John and Lynn Howells. Kevin Bowring had done the decent thing and fallen on his sword. He must have been a bitterly disappointed man, but I'm sure that he passed over the reins with a feeling of relief. The temporary management that took the touring party out to South Africa could not have expected too much in the way of results, but even they could not have foreseen the calamitous match which took place at Pretoria. The Test match was like a training run for the Springboks as they swarmed all over the dispirited Welsh side. The score of 96–13 was a fair reflection of the game, but the Boks could very easily have passed the 100-mark. Our humiliation was complete.

The fans I spoke to were realistic about the result. Very few apportioned the blame to the players. This was simply a tour too far. After twenty-five years of defeat and disappointment, we had grown accustomed to losing. We looked back with nostalgia to that far-off golden era. Our tendency always to look back, to imagine what Gareth and Phil, Gerald and JPR would have done was part, I felt, of our problem. We were missing the point entirely. The game had moved on while Wales, once the innovators who had introduced the concept of squad coaching, had sat back and done nothing. We created pressure for our players, who were constantly compared, unfairly and unfavourably, with their predecessors. In the Welsh team of the '90s, I thought, even the greats of the '70s would have struggled. Now we attended matches with a weary acceptance of our lot.

I was increasingly feeling that I went to internationals through a sense of duty rather than from any passionate commitment. The long journeys to and from Wembley were a chore, and an expensive one at that. Midway through 1998 I had serious doubts about whether I would bother to make the effort in the coming season. But in the build-up to the 1999 season, all that changed. The Welsh nation was given hope by the arrival of one man – Graham Henry. Given our insularity, I doubt that many supporters really knew a great deal about Henry other than what we were told of his successes with Auckland in the Super 12 tournament. At least the WRU was showing some ingenuity in looking abroad for a coach, and where better to look than New Zealand. The other positive was that they were focusing on matters on the field, rather than peripheral issues. Anyway, we were desperate and happy to clutch at any straw that was offered.

From the moment he arrived in Wales, Henry attracted a huge amount of media interest. Henry inspired confidence right from the start. His manner was brusque, and he revealed an extremely dry sense of humour. He didn't spare our feelings when outlining all the things that were wrong with Wales, the Welsh and the national game. He told us in no uncertain terms that we were insular, backward-looking, tribal underachievers – Henry never tried to soft-soap anyone. This sort of talk might have resulted in him being tarred and feathered, but the Welsh supporters could see the truth in his pronouncements and some of us even hoped that the WRU might actually listen to this man.

THE DRAGON AWAKES

We all believed that the straight-talking Kiwi coach might just be the saviour we had been seeking. The media were convinced, and rapidly built up a portrait of Henry as a Messiah of Welsh rugby. Given the propensity of the press to build someone up in order to destroy them at a later date, Graham Henry should have been somewhat nervous. There had, after all, been many false dawns over the last twenty-odd years.

Out of the enthusiasm that Henry inspired grew the idea for this book, and so I spent the next twelve months following the Welsh team through the Five Nations and on to the training camps prior to the World Cup. During this time the team grew in stature, to the extent that by the First of October there was a real belief that they could actually achieve something in the tournament we were to host.

Graham Henry enjoyed an extended honeymoon period with the Welsh public and the media. Although the team's performance in the World Cup was something of a disappointment, the fans stayed loyal. It is probably testament to the importance given to the tournament in the Welsh psyche that it was the team's failure in the newly enlarged Six Nations tournament which resulted in the beginnings of doubt about the man who had been dubbed the Redeemer. Henry's second experience of Home Nations rugby was a pretty stormy one. However, he got through the season bloodied but unbowed, with a Welsh team which is evolving into something that may well start to breathe fire in the coming seasons.

Andrew Williams
October 2000

ONE

ENTER THE REDEEMER

COMETH THE HOUR, COMETH THE MAN. The WRU is not universally liked in Wales. Its committee gets the blame for most things that go wrong in Welsh rugby – everything from poor results to ticketing problems is laid at their door. The relationship between the WRU and the fans is summed up by the comment of one fan on the decision to keep falcons in the new Millennium Stadium. The falcons are to be kept in the ground to discourage pigeons from nesting in the roof of the stadium, as there is a fear that vast numbers of pigeons might take up residence in the roof and defecate on spectators below. When this was discussed prior to the opening match of the World Cup, a fan was heard to say: 'Aye, 'cos we all know that only the WRU are allowed to shit on the fans!' Much of the criticism is probably justified, but it is to their eternal credit that at the darkest hour of Welsh rugby, they pulled out all the stops to get the right man to lead Wales back to the top of the international game.

Graham Henry was widely regarded as one of the top coaches in world rugby. He had led the Auckland Blues to back to back championships in the Super 12 series, involving the best teams in the Southern Hemisphere. Like many top coaches in any sport, Graham Henry's background lies in education. Having earned a Diploma in Physical Education while at university, Henry began a career as a teacher. As he built his professional career, moving up the educational hierarchy, he also began to acquire a reputation as a rugby coach. In the mid-'70s he was responsible for the 1st IV at Auckland Grammar School, and under his guidance the school team was hugely successful, putting together an unbeaten run which extended over two seasons, and winning the secondary school championships. Henry is a man who enjoys challenges, and coaching a successful school team was never going to be enough for him. He has admitted that, even then, he had ambitions to coach Auckland and the All Blacks. In order to achieve this Henry had to put himself on the coaching ladder, and the first step was to become involved at provincial level.

In 1981 Henry became coach of the Auckland University team. The University team was at a pretty low ebb when Henry took it over and he added to his coaching CV by reversing their fortunes quickly. He also gained more useful experience by becoming coach to the New Zealand secondary schools team, whom he took on tour to the UK. In 1985 Henry's professional career reached its peak as he was appointed as headmaster at Kelston Boys' High School. In the same year he took over as coach to the Auckland Colts. Henry's time with the Auckland Colts brought him into contact with a number of future star players, many of whom he would later work with at Auckland. The team included such notables as Inga Tuigamala, Pat Lam, Robin Brooke, Eroni Clarke, Craig Innes, Olo Brown and Craig Dowd. With such talent to work on, Henry's time with the Colts was, not surprisingly, successful and enjoyable. Under his tenure the side won thirty-nine out of forty games.

Finally, in 1992, Henry achieved his first major rugby ambition and was appointed coach of Auckland. For the past few seasons Auckland, under Maurice Trapp and Bryan Williams, had been the major force in New Zealand rugby, but Henry felt that they were beginning to fade, and he was aware of the need for change within the team.

On taking charge at Auckland, Henry's first move was to set up a new management team. His belief in the importance of a strong management team is something that manifested itself again when he eventually took charge of Wales in 1998. Although he is sometimes accused of being autocratic, Henry is too smart to think that one coach can be all things to a team. He believes in bolstering his position through surrounding himself with a strong team of advisers and assistants. He looks for strong-minded, talented aides, people that he can use as sounding boards.

Henry's time at Auckland was not, as many believe, a period of unalloyed success. He had the unenviable task of taking over a successful team, crammed with international stars, many of whom were past their peak. Under his guidance the team lost the Ranfurly Shield, which had been held by the Auckland club for so long that many felt it was theirs by right.

This was not the most auspicious of starts for the new coach and during this time Henry enjoyed a strained relationship with the media, something which seems impossible to those of us who have got to know him as the darling of rugby correspondents in Wales. At this time rugby was still an amateur game, and in addition to holding down the high profile position as coach to the Auckland side, Graham was also working for a living as head teacher at Kelston. Running a school of some 1,250 pupils while masterminding the campaign for the country's leading rugby club put tremendous pressure on Henry.

All of this changed after the World Cup of 1995, when the game went professional. With the advent of professionalism came a new tournament and fresh challenges for the Kelston head teacher. Graham was appointed as coach of the newly formed Auckland Blues, who would compete against sides from

THE DRAGON AWAKES

Australia, New Zealand and South Africa in the new, high-profile, professional tournament. Henry stayed on at Kelston for the first season of the Super 12s, but prior to the second season he decided to commit full time to rugby coaching.

Under Henry, the Auckland Blues won the Super 12 Tournament in its first two seasons. Auckland could boast more than their fair share of star players, most notably greats such as Zinzan Brooke, Sean Fitzpatrick, Jonah Lomu and Michael Jones. It could be argued that with players of that calibre in the team Auckland couldn't lose, but the coach's role in harnessing those talents and making them perform as a team was crucial. In 1998, after Fitzpatrick had retired and Zinzan Brooke had headed off to become player/coach of Harlequins, Auckland Blues still made the Super 12 final and were somewhat unlucky to lose to Canterbury Crusaders. The Auckland Blues dominated the Super 12 competition in its opening years, and Henry had risen through the ranks to become coach of the New Zealand A team as well. His star was in the ascendancy, and his success attracted attention from abroad.

At the end of the 1997 Super 12 season, Henry had been approached by England, with a view to him taking charge of the Under-21 and England A squads, and possibly, at some point, the full national squad. This was stopped by the administrators of the New Zealand game, but a year later Terry Cobner contacted Henry and invited him to become Welsh national coach. The move attracted a lot of flak in New Zealand, where Henry was told that his home union was flatly opposed to him taking his expertise abroad. As a Welshman, it is heartening to see such insecurity at the top of the All Black hierarchy.

Wales offered Henry a five-year contract. Henry had to look at his options; his main ambition, understandably, was to become coach of the All Blacks. In fact, Henry had applied for the post of All Blacks' coach in 1995. Laurie Mains coached the All Blacks to the final of the World Cup in that year. After their surprising defeat by South Africa, Mains decided to give up the reins. Henry and John Hart stood as his replacement.

The post of coach to the national team is filled on the recommendation of a coaching sub-committee. Henry lobbied the characters whom he saw as the opinion-makers in New Zealand rugby, only to find that he should have been lobbying the members of the sub-committee. The post eventually went to Hart, and Henry has said subsequently that Hart's business background carried more clout than his own history in education, but he has great respect for Hart and has even adopted some of his strategies. Hart introduced the idea of players' mentors into the All Black squad. This involved past All Black greats advising the current group of players, an idea that Henry would bring into the Welsh camp during 1999 when he got many of the great names of the '70s involved as technical advisers to the Welsh squad.

In his defeat by Hart in 1995, Henry's campaign showed his lack of political nous in such matters. This failure may have influenced Henry in his decision to take the Welsh job. While the chance of becoming All Black coach remained only a possibility, he was being offered the chance to coach a national side, and so, after much thought, the Auckland coach accepted the offer and prepared to ship to Wales.

The parting from New Zealand proved pretty acrimonious. It was made clear to Henry that if he went abroad, he could kiss goodbye to his chances of ever becoming coach to the All Blacks. The pettiness of this was underlined by the fact that the NZRFU made it clear that their decision was not retrospective – this meant that it wouldn't affect those New Zealanders already coaching abroad. John Mitchell, then assistant coach with England, Warren Gatland of Ireland and Brad Johnstone of Fiji would all still be eligible. Henry appeared to have been singled out for special measures.

Henry's employers at Auckland Rugby Club were similarly

difficult. They demanded NZ$250,000 compensation for the loss of their coach, a sum of money which Henry would have to find from his own pocket. They also took back his entitlement to two tickets and a parking space at their Eden Park ground. It is probably a pointer to the character of the new Welsh coach that not only did he refuse to be bullied by the New Zealand Union, he also refused to lose his sense of humour over the whole issue. His attitude to it all, at least in public, was one of bemused disbelief.

Henry arrived in Wales to a fanfare welcome, which I think took him somewhat by surprise. When, during the summer of 1999, I got to know Graham Henry, we discussed his thoughts on arriving in Wales. He confessed that he had been relatively ignorant of the state of the game in the Principality. If he had been fully versed in the state of play, I wonder if he might have been daunted by the size of the challenge that lay before him. Knowing him reasonably well I doubt it, but there were problems both on and off the field which made his task a momentous one.

I first met Graham when the Welsh squad were at their first training camp in Brecon. We met on the playing fields of Christ College, Brecon, and while the players relaxed after a hard training session, Henry outlined his thoughts on taking the Welsh post. 'The thing that really excited me about the post,' he told me, 'was that Wales is a real rugby nation. Rugby is the national game here, just like it is in New Zealand. It excites great enthusiasm and passion here. If I hadn't been aware of that before, it certainly became apparent on my arrival. Everyone I met wanted to discuss the prospects of the national side, and everybody had an opinion on what was wrong with the Welsh game.'

THE DRAGON AWAKES

Graham Henry is a phlegmatic character, with a wry sense of humour. He gives the impression that nothing fazes him, but he was clearly baffled and somewhat bemused by the attention he had received since coming to Wales: the acclaim he was receiving was of the kind usually reserved for pop stars, and it had made simple daily tasks like going shopping an impossibility. In doing research for this book I spent several weeks with the Welsh squad, and had first-hand experience of the pressures placed on both the players and the coach. It was impossible, even in the security of the team hotel, for Graham to walk across the lobby without his progress being interrupted by numerous well-wishers and pundits with views on how the team should be run.

Graham may have underestimated the intensity of the nation's love of rugby. He may well have also underestimated the magnitude of his task. He told me that while he was aware that Wales had been going through a bad patch, he had not watched videos of their recent games and couldn't even have named many of the current team when he arrived. He must have had no idea of the parlous state of the domestic game below international level, and it is worth a reminder of the situation that faced him as he took the reins.

The WRU were in dispute with Cardiff and Swansea rugby clubs, which resulted in the two leading clubs deserting the national league in order to play a series of friendlies against English clubs. With Cardiff and Swansea out of the frame, the Welsh premiership became even less competitive than it had been. Llanelli, Pontypridd and Ebbw Vale were dominating the reduced competition. Once-great clubs, such as Neath, Bridgend and Newport, were languishing in mid-table, in a league that was at depressingly low ebb. Many leading players had abandoned Welsh rugby to play in England.

The move to professionalism had been far from smooth, even in England, but in Wales it had been a disaster. There simply wasn't sufficient money in the game in Wales to sustain a reasonable number of competitive, professional teams, and there were few entrepreneurs willing to bankroll the clubs. This meant that the level of competitive rugby being played by the leading clubs was well below that required at international level. The Welsh premiership was light years from the Super 12 tournament, which has served to hone the skills of players in the Southern Hemisphere.

Within the national squad there was much factionalism, caused by the fact that there were huge disparities in the wages paid to the players. Some star players were on huge salaries, while others were simply on win bonuses which, as Henry explained, 'didn't amount to a whole lot, the way the team had been playing'. The coaching system within the Welsh set-up was also far from perfect. Players were expected to attend weekly training sessions in Cardiff, which simply disrupted their training regimes at club level and resulted in them spending an inordinate amount of time travelling around Wales.

With club rugby in a state of chaos, the atmosphere in the national team was hardly conducive to producing a team of world-beaters. Henry's first task was to create a stable environment, within which the players could develop and realise their potential, because, as he pointed out: 'Even with my rudimentary knowledge of the game in Wales, I was aware that there were a number of world-class players to draw on.' In the first twelve months of his tenure the media made much of Henry's input, of his coaching methods and his psychological battles with opposing sides. In fact, when one gets close to the squad it becomes apparent that his real masterstroke involved putting together a management team which could create the perfect environment for his players.

His unique management style was apparent on my first meeting with Henry. As we chatted on the side of the playing fields in Brecon, Steve Black, the Welsh fitness coach, put the players through their paces. They ran through a series of moves and plays and I was distracted from our conversation by the fact that there was no ball in evidence. On my first few visits to the Welsh camp, I watched them play rugby without a ball, and also play tennis, squash and cricket; a very different approach to anything I had seen with any other rugby team. Henry, noticing my confused expression, commented: 'Blackie's a one-off. His approach is totally different to anything I've experienced before.'

Black first came to Henry's notice courtesy of a number of Kiwi players based at Newcastle Falcons rugby club. 'I was in England doing a feasibility study on tying in Blackheath RFC as a feeder club for the Auckland Blues. At New Year I went up to Scotland and stopped off in Newcastle to see Pat Lam, Inga Tuigamala and Ross Nesdale, who were over playing for the Falcons. At that time they were the top team in the English league, and when I got together with the lads I asked them what was behind their success. As one, they said "Steve Black". This intrigued me, because it's not normally the fitness coach who gets singled out for that sort of acclaim. Some time later I was out in Apia preparing the New Zealand A team to play Samoa, and I asked Pat Lam again about this guy Black. Well, he just couldn't speak highly enough about him. So when I got the Welsh job, I got in touch with Steve and he agreed to meet me. I met up with him in Bristol, with Terry Cobner, and after about half an hour I had to tell him to shut up so I could get a couple of questions in.'

There is obviously tremendous chemistry between the two men, and their different styles dovetail together perfectly. Henry is the tactician, the analyst who studies the game in tremendous depth. He is the cool, calculating brain behind the Welsh team. Before each match he spends hours painstakingly going through videotapes of the opposition, highlighting their strengths and weaknesses. His preparation is meticulous in every aspect, from training through to working out his game plan for each match. Black, on the other hand, works from the gut. He is a garrulous

Geordie, although he now claims to be naturalised Welsh. He is the motivator of the team and it is evident watching him interact with the players that he is held in great esteem and affection by everyone in the squad.

Black's training techniques are unusual. He works on a psychological level, instilling confidence and commitment in the players as individuals and as a squad. Blackie stresses the importance of a collective commitment to excellence. My first impression on watching the training sessions was that they were relatively easy. The players seemed to enjoy prolonged rest periods, or sessions that involved lighthearted squash and tennis matches. To the casual spectator these sessions don't appear to be geared for high performance athletes preparing for an intensely physical game. However, after regular attendance at a number of sessions, you realise that the overall pattern is to give the players lengthy warm-ups consisting of something more interesting than repeated laps of the pitch, followed by short periods of intense activity. By condensing the activity into short, concentrated bursts, Black is able to place more emphasis on the quality of the effort.

Talking to Blackie is a truly enjoyable experience. He is a man totally dedicated to his work, and is obviously in love with what he does. There is a constant twinkle in his eye and he is chuffed to find someone else taking an interest in his work. What is also evident is that he really cares about the players in his charge. On our first meeting, he outlined his basic plan: 'I get to know the players really well, to know their capabilities, their psychological make-up. I need to understand them, to marry their potential to the dreams they have for themselves, so body, mind and spirit come together.'

My empathy with Black increased when he started talking of the areas he thought critical to the development of a Welsh team: 'From now until the World Cup we'll be paying homage to speed. Speed is a habit. You may have someone who has the potential for speed, but they aren't fast because they get out of the habit. Invariably, what happened when professionalism came into rugby union was that everyone talked about getting fitter, and they spent far too long training from an endurance standpoint. Endurance is not the major thing – the major thing is speed. Endurance doesn't play a part at all, not at the top level in sport. If you've got great endurance but you haven't got speed, you'll never get there. You're always going to be struggling to get back to make the tackle, or to get into a position to take advantage of your positional awareness. If you're habitually active, then stamina comes on the back of that.' Little did we know at the time just how quickly these statements would return to haunt Blackie.

The remainder of the management team that Henry gathered around him consisted of Dai Pickering, Lynn Howells, Allan Lewis and Trevor James. Pickering was a highly respected player with Llanelli and Wales, and now runs his own business. Henry stresses that he has the necessary positive attitude, and being younger, was someone with whom the current crop of players could identify. 'He's been there and done it at the top level,' Henry explained, 'he knows first-hand the problems the players face, and they respect him.' Howells is another hugely respected figure. He was the forwards' coach at Pontypridd, a club whose reputation is based on hard, unrelenting forward play. Pontypridd are constantly referred to as 'unfashionable' and Howells had to work with the minimum of resources, making the best of the limited assets at his disposal – a perfect preparation for working with the beleaguered Welsh team. He is now head coach at Cardiff, and has finally made the nation's biggest club start to punch its weight.

Both Pickering and Howells contribute hugely to the positive, workmanlike yet relaxed atmosphere that surrounds the current Welsh team. Both men work the players hard, but at the same time stress the fun element of the game in the same way as Black and Henry.

The Dragon Awakes

Lewis is head coach at Newport and is responsible for the backs' coaching within the national squad. He is a quieter and more retiring character, but enjoys the respect of all those involved in the game at the highest level. Trevor James has been the administrator of the Welsh team for years. Henry felt that he brought an element of continuity into the management set-up. He knows his way around, and is used to dealing with the politics that surround rugby in the Principality.

With the management team in place, Henry set about putting together a team which could do the business on the field. He told me later that keeping a distance from the recent past of the Welsh team was crucial at this stage. 'I deliberately didn't look at any old videos of club or international matches,' he told me prior to the Five Nations, 'because I thought that would be a negative step. I didn't want to have any preconceived ideas. I had been coaching for twenty-five years when I came to Wales, so I know what I'm looking to build. I didn't want to cloud that by worrying about what had happened in the recent past. I wanted to make a clean start, and I wanted the players to have a fresh start as well. I had a vision of the type of team, the type of player that I wanted. I then tried to find the kind of players in Wales who could fulfil my vision of how I wanted the game to be played. I made a few mistakes along the way: Garin Jenkins would be a prime example. I didn't think he had the athletic capabilities to play the type of game I wanted to develop, but I underestimated his psychological importance to the team. He is a tremendous scrummager and a great motivator for the other seven in the pack. He's a top team man and the rest of the guys think the world of him. I got it wrong, and I learnt from the experience.' This is typical of Henry: his cool assurance belies a willingness to learn and an ability to admit his mistakes and benefit from them.

In August, players were invited to take part in a series of trial games. These matches served a dual purpose: they gave Henry the opportunity to run his eye over the top sixty or so players in Wales, and they also sent a message to the players that places were up for grabs. What type of player, I asked Graham at this early stage in his reign, was he hoping the trials would turn up? 'The game has changed in the last few years,' he told me. 'The law changes, especially in the lineout, have resulted in the need for more dynamism. Today's game is based on retention of possession and keeping the ball in hand. Players need to be quick to the breakdown, and they must be able to recycle possession quickly. For this sort of game you need athletic, thinking players, players with good ball skills.' There is a shortage of this type of player in Wales, and Henry stressed the need for a change in attitude amongst our players and coaches. 'You know yourself,' he said, 'in training sessions here coaches spend much of their time going through set piece play – scrummaging and lineout work take up an inordinate amount of time at club training sessions. How many lineouts are there in a game – twenty-five, thirty? How many scrums – eighteen, twenty? By comparison, how many tackle situations are there? Possibly eighty or more. We should be focusing our attention on the tackle area. The modern game is won by the team that can recycle the ball quickly from ruck and maul, and keep the game alive. Another negative aspect of the way rugby is played here is that the game is far more physical than it is in New Zealand. Welsh players are always looking for contact, often to the detriment of their game. Alongside this there is a lack of discipline. I couldn't believe the number of fights I saw in the first dozen or so club games I watched. We need a change in approach.'

Before and after the trials Henry spent much of his time touring the clubs throughout Wales, getting to know the players and the coaches. This was more than just a public relations exercise. 'I felt it was important. I wanted everyone involved to know what I was trying to achieve. I stressed that I was not simply extolling the virtues of the All Black way, and also I needed to know what players were doing at club level in order to prepare them for the step up to international football. I was pleased by the quality of players available, but I wasn't very happy with the way top players were being prepared. What with club commitments and regular squad sessions, the top players were being asked to do too much. I did away with the weekly sessions and ran two training camps in October in preparation for my first Test, South Africa. The first of these was another revelation: the players lacked a sense of urgency, and there was no zip in anything they did. Everything was done at about 70 per cent speed. I want the players to give their all during training. This not only makes it more fun, it also prepares them for the pace at which they are going to have to play international rugby. After I had been in Wales for a while someone asked me what the difference between a New Zealand player and a Welsh one was. I had to think for a while, but finally I told him that at the age of one there is no difference between a New Zealand and a Welsh child, but they develop differently. New Zealanders do everything more quickly, while the Welsh are more laid-back. An admirable trait, but not one that is wanted in an international rugby player.'

It seemed to me that Henry's task involved more than simply getting the best out of a team which was under-performing – he needed to transform the working ethos of players at the top level. It was a massive task to alter an approach which had been ingrained into players over generations. How did he set about making the necessary changes? 'I had to work on three levels: improving fitness, perfecting skills and developing mental discipline. The first of these is Blackie's responsibility. He has the expertise and knows a good deal more than me. We discuss general requirements and then I leave it up to him to implement a schedule, knowing that he will deliver the goods. The other two areas are interwoven. Obviously, after a run of bad results the players' morale and self esteem is not at its highest. However,

THE DRAGON AWAKES

I was aware that there was a pool of experienced world-class players. I felt I had to let them take on responsibility for their own development. The players need to be bold, to make the shift from hoping things will happen to making things happen. I also noticed that there was a tendency to kick away possession; generally speaking, players kick away possession in the hope that the opposition will stuff it up, and that stems from a negative mindset and a lack of confidence. I had to make the guys more positive. Giving players their head is crucial in this respect: they need the confidence to make decisions, to go forward with the ball in hand and be bold.'

The magnitude of his task in ringing these changes is emphasised by Henry's belief that this negative mindset may well be something of a national trait. 'There are probably historical reasons for this, but I feel that we, the Welsh nation, are followers rather than leaders. It may be because for years we have been dominated by the English. What we have to do is develop leadership qualities: initiative, self-confidence and decision-making capabilities. A good rugby player is the guy who shows initiative and makes things happen, rather than waiting for something to happen. When you've got fifteen guys like that you're starting to get a rugby team together. Steve Black is awesome in developing this. He builds a player's self-esteem up and then puts the onus on him to realise his potential. That is the way his fitness routines are devised. He gives the players guidelines about the tasks they have to do, but after that they have to fill in the gaps and use their own initiative.' It is ironic that the Welsh nation has taken to its heart a man who doesn't hesitate to point out the weaknesses in our national character. He tells it like it is, and paints a portrait of us warts and all – and we love him for it.

In Wales's last game before Henry took over they had been overwhelmed by a rampant South African side and suffered a record defeat. In mitigation, it has to be said that it was a weakened Welsh side which toured South Africa that summer. Many leading players were not available for the tour, and the entire enterprise was another illustration of the unsustainable treadmill which international rugby has become. The summer of 1997 had seen the hugely enjoyable Lions series in South Africa. The top players in the UK were obviously thrilled to have been a part of that momentous tour, but they had then returned home to a full domestic season at club and international level. Summer tours in 1998 obviously carried the risk of players being over-played. With that in mind England rested many star players for their tour to Australia, and suffered a consequent hammering by the Australians. The English also suffered a great deal of criticism for sending a sub-standard team on tour. While I can understand the disappointment of the Australian Rugby Union at having a deliberately weakened side sent for what was billed as a major tour, I think that the English were being longsighted and sensible in resting a number of key players. The Welsh squad selection didn't attract as much media condemnation as the English had, but the squad was weakened for exactly the same reason. In addition, Wales toured under new management, seen as a caretaker regime which was just plugging a gap while the WRU sought to find a replacement for Kevin Bowring. All in all the team that went to take on the world champions on their home patch was far from being a strong, settled group. The poor results were to be expected. Nevertheless, the squad that convened in the autumn under the new coach contained some pretty battered egos, which had been badly bruised by the disastrous tour in South Africa.

Obviously, Graham's first task was to shore up a more than fragile defence. 'Yes,' he told me, 'the backbone of any rugby side is its ability to defend, and that has a lot to do with attitude, with character, guts and determination. My prime objective before we play South Africa is to strengthen our defence so that they don't score against us. We need good defensive patterns, good communication and a willingness to lay our bodies on the line. Building this revolves around making use of the experienced players in the squad. Rob Howley is a natural choice as skipper; it was an easy decision to stick with him. Apart from being a world-class player, he has the respect of the team and his captaincy brings an element of continuity into the equation. His job is made easier by the wealth of experience around him, guys like Garin Jenkins, David Young, Colin Charvis, Scott Quinnell, Neil Jenkins, Scott Gibbs and Allan Bateman. These guys have been around and they know what's needed at the highest level. They are complete professionals. They help to instil the right attitude in the less experienced players. Developing the leadership qualities of the senior players is the key to developing a positive team ethos.'

Henry's cause was certainly helped by the return of a number of players who had gone north over the past few years. Dai Young, Scott Quinnell and Allan Bateman brought a wealth of experience to the squad, as well as the professionalism they developed in the hard world of rugby league. Rugby union was beginning to adapt to life as a professional sport and was moving away from the boozy image of its past. Allan Bateman noticed radical changes when he returned: 'Everything is more focused now. Training is more specific and is taken a great deal more seriously than it was in the amateur days. Players are expected to behave in a more professional way, both on and off the field. The players in the current squad have bought into the professional ethos completely, and under Graham there is a far greater awareness of the need to work at pace. Fitness levels are higher than ever before, and Graham has instilled an air of confidence and self-belief in the team, something which has been decidedly lacking in recent years.'

Henry's first hurdle as Welsh coach was the game against South Africa. Playing the world champions is never easy, and coming on the back of the disastrous result in South Africa the previous summer, this was a major task. However, a number of factors aided Henry in his preparations for the game. Firstly, there was the 'new broom' syndrome. There was a feeling in the camp that everyone was being given a fresh start and the players were all very keen and enthusiastic at the beginning of what was being seen as a new era.

Ironically, the schism in Welsh domestic rugby also aided the cause: Cardiff and Swansea had seceded from the WRU and were playing matches against the clubs in England's Allied Dunbar Premiership. Games against the likes of Bath and Leicester meant that a fair proportion of Wales's leading players were, at long last, playing truly competitive rugby. As the season progressed, however, these matches became increasingly meaningless, as the English clubs used them as an opportunity to blood new young players. But at this stage, the supposed 'friendlies' against top English clubs were being taken seriously by everyone and this significantly strengthened the Welsh squad. In addition, the home-based players were involved in the European Cup, and regular games against the top sides in France and the rest of Europe exposed them to a higher standard of football.

However, the new coach also encountered a number of problems in the build-up to the game. At his first training session he was struck by the lack of urgency amongst the players. This was Henry's first encounter with what he came to call the 'Plod Syndrome'. He noted that, in training, players walked from one phase to the next. There was no urgency, no fizz, in their actions. Training sessions tend to take place at half-pace, with no one committing themselves 100 per cent to the drills. Henry puts this down to overplaying – he believes that our players spend too much time playing and training and consequently they are never able to give more than 80 per cent in any given situation. This remains a problem at all levels of the game. While the WRU has acknowledged Henry's statement that the number of games needs to be reduced, the problem remains. The better players, even at Under-11 level, are playing in excess of forty games per year. From the moment he took over the Welsh team Henry has stressed the need for fewer games and a higher standard. What he had inherited in Wales was a squad of players reduced to drudges by overwork.

Henry's other difficulty on taking over the Welsh team was his unfamiliarity with the culture of rugby in Wales. From the outset, he made himself accessible to everybody with an opinion concerning the Welsh team. Unfortunately, what he didn't realise was that, in Wales, this represents 90 per cent of the population. What Henry failed to appreciate at first was just how parochial Welsh supporters are. As a nation of rugby supporters we are, for the most part, completely one-eyed. Pontypridd supporters lobby for a Welsh team consisting largely of players from Sardis Road. Llanelli's faithful are safe in the knowledge that 90 per cent of the Scarlets' team should also be donning the red shirt of Wales. We at Ebbw Vale constantly bemoan the lack of judgement of the selectors who persist in ignoring the claims of players at Eugene Cross Park. Retrospectively, Graham Henry was aware that because he listened to too many differing opinions, a number of players didn't feature in his thoughts as quickly as they should have.

Henry's first team selection showed no radical changes from recent Welsh outfits. 'I had stressed that I wanted a degree of continuity and stability, and this was reflected in my team selection,' he told me. 'Since my arrival I had spent considerable time travelling the country, absorbing as much Welsh rugby as possible. I didn't limit my travels to the Principality, but spent time in England watching Welsh qualified players at clubs like Richmond and London Welsh. I very quickly singled out some players as potential keys to the building of the new Welsh team. The return of world-class players such as Scott Gibbs, Allan Bateman and Scott Quinnell not only gave us greater depth, they also brought a professional attitude and discipline to the team, which is crucial in the modern era. Scott Quinnell's younger brother Craig impressed me as a powerful ball-carrying forward with the potential to inflict enormous damage on opposing defences. His partner in the second row for the South African game was Chris Wyatt. Wyatt played at number 8 for his club, Llanelli, but as an athletic, ball-playing second row, he brought another dimension to our game. The absence of the hugely experienced Dai Young and Peter Rogers meant that I was forced to select an inexperienced front five against the reigning world champions. One possibly controversial selection was that of Shane Howarth at full-back. I knew Shane well, having coached him at Auckland. He gained four caps for the All Blacks back in 1994, before moving to rugby league. I had been told of his Welsh heritage before I left New Zealand. John Mitchell, the Kiwi coach at Sale, had told me that Shane still had an appetite for international rugby. Apart from his undoubted football skills, Shane brought a hugely positive attitude into the camp: he exudes confidence, and is a thorough professional. Having worked so closely with him at Auckland, I had no doubts as to his value to the team.'

Henry has developed a reputation as a player of mind games, and he evidently enjoys unsettling opponents during the build-up to matches. This time, the Welsh public had no reason to doubt his word when he told us not to expect too much in the forthcoming Test. Wales were, he said, very definitely the underdogs, and victory was not expected. In reality Graham was pleased to promote this lack of expectancy, and he used it to advantage in gearing the players up for the Test ahead. As he told me later: 'There had been much talk of the hammering the Welsh boys had suffered at the hands of the Springboks earlier in the year. While that result did nothing to foster confidence in the Welsh camp, I was able to play down its significance as that team had been badly weakened by a few key absences. It also served to deflect the pressure of expectation away from the team. The Welsh are a passionate nation, and that passion is particularly evident in their support of the national team. This can be a great bonus, but it also brings pressure, at times unbearable, on to the players. Nobody, not even the most fervent Welsh supporter, thought we had a realistic chance against the world champions, and the role of underdog was one that suited our purpose. There may have been little expectation on the part of the Welsh public, but I hadn't come to Wales to coach a losing side. I genuinely thought we could win the game.' This was a new beginning and a new Welsh team.

Henry's optimism was almost proved correct. Once again, thousands of Welsh supporters made the lengthy trek to our temporary home in North London. On the train the mood was hopeful, but although the faithful fans had respect for the new coach we didn't expect miracles, even from the man hailed as 'the Redeemer'. We hoped for a respectable loss, rather than a miraculous victory. An hour later we were euphoric, though shamefaced at our lack of faith.

Wales got off to a dream start under the new leader. The Welsh team was bold and aggressive. From the moment Shane Howarth ran a tapped penalty in his own twenty-two, the crowd started to believe and as we went into the final quarter, we were leading 20–17. There was a dreamlike quality about the match: surely this could not really be happening! We were deservedly ahead and the all-powerful Springboks were on the ropes. Suddenly, the jeering Afrikaaners were muted and thoughtful. The unfamiliarity of this situation also seemed to have an effect on the Welsh players, who seemed to freeze at the enormity of what they might be about to achieve. A streaker, presumably South African, invaded the pitch and the players seemed to lose their focus – the South Africans came back and snatched a victory. As Graham had told me before the match, winning is a habit. Evidently it was a habit which the Welsh team still needed to acquire, and one with which the Springboks were well acquainted.

The Welsh nation was euphoric about our near-victory. For the first time in what seemed like an age, we had a side that could compete with the best in the world. The team had more zip and fire than any of us had imagined possible. Obviously Graham Henry was behind this transformation, but much of the credit went to Shane Howarth. A new Welsh favourite had arrived. Throughout the game Shane was electric, bristling with confidence and inventiveness, and this seemed to rub off on those around him.

This was a hugely positive game despite the result, but for Henry it was not enough. He was happy with much of the Welsh effort, but for him it served to highlight our deficiencies. In his post-match summary he said: 'A critical refereeing decision just before half-time resulted in a penalty try, which allowed the Boks back into the game. We lost our edge towards the end of each half, and failed to maintain our intensity. This reflected our lack of fitness and our lack of adequate competition at club level. There was a lack of self-discipline in the last ten minutes of the game, which was unprofessional and cost us the game. We lost the match, rather than South Africa winning it. Despite that, there were a lot of positives to be taken from the game: we played with attitude and produced a positive, quality performance both in attack and defence, marred by a few weak points.'

The players realised how close they had been to winning against the Springboks, and the disappointment they felt sparked a collective desire to produce a positive performance in the next game, against Argentina at Stradey Park. The South African game served to cement the new-found feeling of confidence in the Welsh camp. There were very positive vibes going into the game, and an expectation that Wales should win the game easily. Argentina have a reputation for being a strong, forward-dominated side. Their game revolves around a strong scrummaging pack, but their back division is far from the best. With the Welsh public convinced that victory was inevitable, there was a danger that we would become overconfident. I was concerned that we might slip up as a result of this. I needn't have worried. In the game against Argentina, they played in the same bold, aggressive, attacking style which they had adopted in the first sixty minutes against the Boks. In some ways the result was more important than the performance this time, and a 43–30 victory got Wales back into its old winning ways. Graham was pleased, but not exactly happy with the team's display: 'Our defensive display was less satisfactory than at Wembley, and we were badly exposed in the scrum. On occasion we were overconfident and attacked from deep, only to lose possession and give away tries. What was lacking was a sense of balance, a lack of judgement over when to attack and when to play the percentages.'

Generally, though, the two matches had a positive effect. Both performances generated confidence, both amongst the players and in the nation as a whole. The Argentinians had exposed weaknesses in our scrum. This is not exactly remarkable, considering that the Argentinians had probably the strongest scrum in world rugby at that time. Overall, the feeling after these two games was positive, and as the New Year came round there was a strong belief that this year we would be a force to be reckoned with in the Five Nations tournament.

Once again the players returned to their clubs and got back to the weekly round of league games. By Christmas the league structure was obviously not fulfilling its purpose of preparing players for the rigours of international rugby. The Anglo–Welsh friendlies involving Cardiff and Swansea were being taken less seriously by the English clubs, and the league matches were generally of a pretty low standard. Involvement in Europe was over for many of the Welsh clubs and the standard of

The Dragon Awakes

competition was generally too low for Henry's purposes. Although there were comments to this effect in the media, for most people they were forgotten in the excitement of the dawning of another Home International season.

TWO

The Five Nations

FOR EVERY RUGBY PLAYER OR FAN, the Five Nations is the highpoint of the season. It has become an institution which is about more than rugby, yet which never slips into rampant nationalism. As a Welsh rugby supporter, you are indoctrinated from childhood. International weekends are marked on the calendar, and whether you are going to the game or watching it at home, with Bill McLaren on the box, there is always a near-religious ritualism about match days, with which nothing can interfere. It is an eight-week rugby festival, where the social side of the game and the travel to foreign climes have achieved a mythical status amongst the faithful.

The biennial trips to Dublin, Edinburgh, Paris and Twickenham are an integral part of the calendar for all Welsh supporters. Of all these trips, those to Dublin and Edinburgh are the most special. In London and Paris the visiting army of supporters can easily be lost amongst the local population, but when visiting Ireland and Scotland the fans take over the city. There is also an empathy between the celtic supporters which is missing with the English and the French. Graham Henry experienced this for the first time in

The Dragon Awakes

1999. The phenomenon took him completely by surprise.

Our opening game was against Scotland at Murrayfield, always a popular trip, but this year the anticipation was heightened by a sense of expectancy. We had become accustomed to travelling to matches in defeatist mood but this year, following the positive performances in the autumn, there was a great feeling of confidence amongst the travelling support. Suddenly everybody wanted to be a part of the rejuvenated Welsh team, and an estimated twenty thousand supporters made the trek northwards. Graham was flabbergasted by the level of support: 'The Home International tournament is the jewel in the crown. We always follow it avidly in the Southern Hemisphere, but this is the first time I've seen it close up. The intensity of the rivalry between the competing nations and the enthusiasm of the fans is a real eye-opener. When we arrived in Edinburgh, it felt as if the entire nation had travelled with us. In rugby terms at least, the Welsh are a nation of extremes. Two promising results in the autumn had transformed the all-pervasive attitude of despair, which had followed the massacre in Pretoria, into a feeling of near-invincibility.'

The change was certainly evident amongst the travelling fans on Princes Street before the match. Their confidence and self-belief was similar to that which I had observed on visits to the Scottish capital in the mid-'70s. Everybody, media and fans alike, treated the result as a foregone conclusion. Wales were once again a force in the land. The Scots just wouldn't be able to stay with the team who had pushed South Africa so hard in the autumn. Scotland were rank outsiders for the championship, and even the Welsh players must have felt that they were in for an easy victory. There were some worries for Henry as the match approached. Allan Bateman was injured, as was Dai Young, both influential members of the team and there were concerns over the scrummaging of Chris Anthony and Andrew Lewis. However, I think that even Henry was feeling confident of our chances.

The Dragon Awakes

As many international teams, especially the English can testify, you underestimate the Scots at your peril! We were punished for our overconfidence in the opening moments of the game. With the Welsh forwards lined up on the right of the pitch to receive the kick-off, Scotland went left and caught us napping. John Leslie gathered the ball in front of the unsuspecting Matthew Robinson and ran in what must have been the quickest score in international rugby. This hushed the Welsh crowd and caused a severe dent in our new-found confidence, but despite this early setback the players rallied and fought their way back into the game. For the most part, Wales had the best of the match but were unable to dominate. There was a growing feeling that today was not to be our day, highlighted when Rob Howley took a quick tap and the Scots failed to retreat the required ten yards, yet the referee let play go. The ball was turned over and Scotland scored.

On balance, I felt the Scots deserved their 33–20 victory. We let the game slip at crucial points and the players lacked the zip and verve they had displayed against South Africa. Supporters in the bars that evening were divided between those who pessimistically maintained that we had seen yet another false dawn and those who took a more pragmatic approach and asserted that this was just a blip, we shouldn't expect too much too soon.

After the game, Henry was forthright in taking much of the responsibility for the result. He told me: 'The game was hugely overhyped and the expectations were unreal. We allowed ourselves to be lulled into a false sense of security. I should have played this down and made sure the players kept their feet on the ground, but I wasn't prepared for the fervour and intensity of the event. The Five Nations was a steep learning curve for me. Our mindset was wrong going into the game, but there were other factors which contributed to us losing the game. A number of key players, Allan Bateman, David Young, Jonathan Humphreys and

The Dragon Awakes

Gareth Thomas, were carrying injuries. The freshness which was so apparent in the autumn Tests had been dissipated by five months of domestic rugby. The Anglo–Welsh friendlies between Cardiff, Swansea and the top English clubs had fizzled out, and were now fairly meaningless contests. The other Welsh clubs were playing in the Challenge Trophy, which involved games against visiting sides who were generally understrength and under-committed. In reality, there was precious little competitive rugby being played and this was terrible preparation for a series of international matches.' But Henry felt that Wales's problems were more deep-seated than that: 'In the development of a team,' he explained, 'it is crucial that everyone buys into the general plan. I thought that I had achieved this with Wales, but in the emotional intensity of this tournament they fell back into their old habits and lost the edge that they had displayed in the earlier matches. I was also guilty of lacking confidence in some players who, I felt, lacked experience at this level. For example, I shouldn't have played Jonathan Humphreys, who was struggling with a lower back hernia, while I underestimated Garin Jenkins's value as a player and as a top team person. I selected David Young despite the fact that he was struggling to get 100 per cent fit. To be honest, I underestimated the importance in the Welsh psyche of the Home Internationals. The atmosphere surrounding the event is momentous and I had failed to take this on board.'

The Welsh lack of expectation when we took on South Africa in the autumn had worked in our favour, and the Scotland game proved yet again that Wales work best as the underdogs. We went into our next match, against Ireland at Cardiff, as firm favourites. The Scotland game had been a one-off and the rugby public in Wales were certain that the Redeemer would get things right in his second Five Nations game. As a nation we do not learn easily from experience, and once again the optimistic side of our nature was apparent in the build-up to the Ireland game.

The Welsh love the Irish – they are uncomplicated and we

know what to expect. Even in this era of professionalism, the Irish have continued to play with an almost amateur sense of enjoyment. The *craic* off the field is as important as what happens on the pitch. There is always plenty of fire and fury from their forwards and the odd flash of brilliance, but this is generally unsustained and as long as we could weather the early storm, we could soon impose control on the game and victory would be ours. In this analysis, we generally chose to forget the number of times we have come unstuck against them. Even in the glory days of the '70s, we had often gone to Lansdowne Road as favourites, en route for a Triple Crown or a Grand Slam, only to return home defeated. Like us, the Irish relish the role of underdog, and in the second Test of the Five Nations they once again stole in and took the spoils.

The problems highlighted by the Irish game were different to those thrown up in Murrayfield two weeks earlier. The team's principal failing was lack of discipline. Graham Henry had told me that he was struck by the physicality of the Welsh game, and I have often felt that Welsh players at all levels tend to look for confrontation unnecessarily. And so it was against the Irish. In the wake of the defeat, Graham told me what had gone wrong: 'We self-destructed,' he said. 'We lacked discipline, composure and maturity. Lack of discipline was the major factor in us losing the game. It alienated the referee, and rightly so, and as a result 50/50 decisions invariably went in Ireland's favour. This self-destruction is a major worry to me: I am coming to the conclusion that it is an integral part of the Welsh culture. Aggression is an essential part of any rugby player's game, but it must be controlled aggression. There is a tendency for Welsh players to look for the hit unnecessarily. Too often the heart rules the head and composure and discipline go out of the window. Against Ireland we went completely over the top in the first half, and it cost us the match.'

Typically, Graham took the onus of responsibility for not

curbing this over-aggressive approach. 'In the pre-match build-up, I placed too much emphasis on the power and physical presence of the Irish forwards. I stressed that we would need to fight fire with fire. This philosophy exploded in my face. Retrospectively, this was apparent in training: even then, we were allowing the physical side of our game to dominate the thinking process instead of the other way round. The other problem that was becoming apparent was that under pressure, the players were quite simply not doing as they were told. The policies we worked out in training were not being enacted on the field.'

For the supporters there was an overwhelming feeling of *déjà vu*. We really are our own worst enemies. A couple of good results and we suddenly become world-beaters, then the bubble bursts and we are wallowing in despair. It appeared to all but a few that, even under Graham Henry, we were on the familiar roller-coaster ride of boom and bust. Many were quick to point out that under Graham there had been more bust than boom: a good performance against South Africa had still resulted in defeat and a victory over Argentina was no great shakes, given that we still, arrogantly, view the Argentinians as a second-rate rugby nation.

To us winning the Five Nations is what it's really about, and here we were bottom of the table once again! I must admit to being guilty of my fair share of lack of faith at this point. I had booked to go to France in the autumn, when everything seemed rosy. When March came around I had lost the desire and a weekend in Paris watching a heavy Welsh defeat didn't appeal at all. My mind went back to Wembley the preceding year, and memories of the way the rapier-like attacks of the French backs had ripped Wales apart. My wife's attitude, 'you've paid so you're bloody well going', was all that got me on the train for Paris. I really owe her for that.

While we supporters have the freedom to wallow in despair,

the players and the coach have to address the situation in a far more positive manner. The Welsh squad was strangely upbeat in the build-up to the game. There was an air of self-belief in the camp, and the players seemed content in the role of underdogs once again as the game approached. Graham said later that the two defeats did serve a purpose: they forced the players to reassess and refocus. The Scottish and Irish games highlighted our weaknesses, and the squad spent the time between games working on these weak points.

Talking after the match, Graham said, 'During the period following the Irish game, the squad progressed enormously. After much soul-searching by players and management, we went into the French game with a different approach. There was never any danger of overconfidence in the match. Wales had not won in Paris for over twenty years. In our preparations we focused on the mental rather than the physical aspects of our game. I stressed that discipline was paramount, to the extent that players were warned that their future international careers depended on them maintaining discipline at all times. I also stressed the need to stick to the game plan. I felt that against the French, overconfidence was not a problem: the players needed the confidence to take the game to the French – they must be bold. They had to take the opposition on and have the self-belief to try things. If we were apprehensive, we would lose.'

Henry had made some significant team changes since the Irish game. He had come to realise the importance to the team of Garin Jenkins, who came into the team packing down between Peter Rogers and Ben Evans. The front row was something of a gamble: Rogers had played only one full game prior to the international. He had suffered a ligament injury and was still struggling to get match fit, and Ben Evans was hugely talented, but untried at this level of competition. Another controversial change was the inclusion of Brett Sinkinson at open-side flanker. Sinkinson brought a hard edge to the Welsh defence, but the inclusion of another Kiwi caused some comment amongst the press. As far as the press were concerned a win in Paris was out of the question.

Graham Henry was taking a more positive approach. He made one important tactical change for the French match. Neil Jenkins has endured more than his fair share of criticism from the Welsh public and the press. This stems from the fact that he is not a typical, jinking, quicksilver fly-half in the mould of previous greats from Cliff Morgan to Phil Bennett. He is not a breaking fly-half and back-row forwards tend to ignore him and put pressure on the players outside him. Henry noticed that this had been the case against Scotland and Ireland, and decided to change things against the French. In Paris Neil was told to make breaks, which he did to great effect. With Jenkins getting over the gain line, the Welsh midfield had more space to attack the French, who were immediately on the back foot. This exposed a defensive weakness in the French backline, which Graham had noted in their previous matches.

Everything Henry had done was vindicated by the result. On the morning of 6 March I wandered around central Paris taking in the sights, with no real appetite for the match. Lunching in the sun-soaked squares around Notre Dame, it was very tempting to stay in town and savour the atmosphere of the French capital. Eventually my sense of duty prevailed and I took the Métro out to the stadium.

The train ride was a sober affair – evidently other Welsh supporters shared my lack of faith. Fortunately, our lacklustre approach to the game was not shared by the players, who tore into the French voraciously from the kick-off. The match has now passed into Welsh folklore and become one of Max Boyce's 'I was there' moments. In years to come, if you believe all Welshmen, you would think the crowd must have numbered hundreds of thousands – none of whom ever doubted the result!

The Stade de France is a magnificent ground, and it gave us a foretaste of what we would experience when, or if, our own controversial Millennium Stadium was finally completed. Even in the top tier of the ground I had a magnificent view. The seats slope steeply down to the pitch, and make you feel close to the action. On the day, the rugby matched the surroundings and we witnessed a breathtaking display of rugby. The weather was beautiful; hot and sunny, just the way the French like it. The atmosphere was terrific. There were spontaneous eruptions of fireworks, brass bands played throughout the game, and the hypnotic, pounding rhythm of drums echoed around the ground. There was also the inevitable invasion of cockerels on to the pitch.

Welsh club sides playing in France in European competitions have experienced considerable trouble with aggressive, tribal French support. At international level this intimidatory behaviour disappears, and the fans seem intent on celebrating the joy of French rugby. In my section of the crowd the French were jovial and friendly, and very generous with their supply of limitless quantities of red wine. From the start, Wales took the game to the French and we saw the fruit of Graham's exhortations to the players to be bold. After only five minutes Colin Charvis crossed for a try. Jenkins's conversion, added to his third minute penalty, gave us an unbelievable 10–0 lead. Ntamack scored two breathtaking tries, but Wales answered with tries by Dafydd James and Craig Quinnell, and as Jenkins and Castaignède traded penalties we forced ourselves into a winning position.

The first half passed in a flash, and by half-time Wales were leading 18–28. The Welsh supporters were euphoric. The Welsh play had been so positive that I felt we couldn't lose this one. In fact, I was so confident that I even took a bet with the Frenchman sitting next to me: if France won he would have my Welsh jersey, if Wales won I would acquire his beret. The second half was less positive, as Wales lost some of their impetus and allowed France to fight their way back into the game. The French outscored us to take a two-point lead with ten minutes left.

The final ten minutes were the most intense I have experienced in international rugby. Jenkins restored our lead with a penalty and the Welsh defence withstood wave upon wave of desperate French attack. In injury time, Wales went offside at a ruck and Castaignède had a penalty to win the match. My heart sank as the ball headed for the posts. To have got so near to a historic victory only to have it snatched away at the death seemed harsh. Then the ball drifted wide and referee Jim Fleming blew for time. We had made it: 33–34! The remainder of the day remains something of a blur, but as we toured the bars of central Paris, I was able to proudly wear my new French beret.

On the journey home the Welsh supporters were bleary-eyed and hungover. Everybody seemed slightly dazed, and there was a collective feeling of disbelief at what we had just witnessed. On the train from Paddington to Newport those unfortunates who had only watched the game on television quizzed the lucky few who'd been there about the game, and another victory started to assume legendary proportions.

When I met up with Graham, his post-match analysis was rather more sober and studied than mine: 'Well, it was a game of two halves – there's an incisive comment! In the first half we played to plan, but in the second period we lost our way somewhat. As the game wore on we lost our boldness; we turned the ball over at crucial breakdowns and the French came back at us. I was aware there was a distinct possibility that we would self-destruct again. Our lack of fitness was exposed in the later stages, but we held out. This was a huge step forward in terms of the development of the team and probably the most satisfying moment in my coaching career to date. It was a marvellous achievement. I could feel myself getting emotional as the final whistle went.'

The press, too, were unstinting in their praise of Henry's

team. In fact, when the management team entered the post-match press conference, they were given a round of applause by the gathered journalists. Wales had played rugby of which no one had thought them capable. This was Super 12-style football, and they had had the temerity to play it in Paris, at the home of the side thought to be the strongest in Europe.

Two weeks later Henry took the team off to Italy for a friendly, aimed as a dry run for Italy's entry into the Home International tournament next season. The game was seen as something of a sideshow, and had the potential for being a banana skin for the newly confident Welsh squad. If we slipped back into our old weakness of overconfidence we could suffer an embarrassing defeat, and nothing but a comprehensive victory would do. In fact, the players took the game very seriously and we won with something to spare. Wales played skilful, attacking rugby and took full advantage of mistakes by the opposition. By the time the final whistle went we had scored 60 points, with Gareth Thomas running in four tries.

The win in Italy was good for the confidence of the squad and underlined the more resolutely professional approach of the team, but in the context of the next match it was perceived as being of little significance. Our last match of the season was against England, a huge challenge. Could Wales demonstrate that the win in Paris was anything more than a fluke? England were perceived as being the strongest team in the Northern Hemisphere, and they had beaten us convincingly the previous year. The game would be a clear indicator of just how much progress we had made under Graham Henry.

The significance of the game to the Welsh was underlined in the build-up to the match. The Stereophonics, a Welsh rock group, released a track entitled 'As long as we beat the English', and this was used by the BBC in the television build-up. Members of the English media overreacted and attacked the song for being racist, but in fact, the song is partly self-deprecating in its allusion to our preoccupation with beating our nearest and historically dominant neighbour. The song light-heartedly underlines the parochialism of rugby in Wales. Graham Henry was slightly bemused by this attitude. He assured me that while the game was crucial to the development of the team, it was not his intention to be content with beating England regularly. For him, success would only be realised when Wales could regularly compete with the leading nations in both hemispheres. For the rest of us, for the time being at least, a victory over the English would be enough!

Wembley in March turned out to be another glory day. As in Paris, the weather was fine and sunny, the conditions perfect for free-running, attacking rugby. The English crowd was full of confidence and arrogantly discounted our chances of defeating the English machine. England were simply too strong up front, they told us. Dallaglio and company would blast us off the pitch. This attitude seemed to be shared by the English team, who paid dearly for not taking us seriously. This is one of the reasons for the animosity between English and Welsh supporters. The Irish and the Scots share, with the Welsh, a self-deprecating sense of humour, both in defeat and victory. The French, the New Zealanders and the Australians are all magnanimous in victory. The English and the South Africans, on the other hand, share a slighting disregard for any team they beat. In return, the Welsh tend to gloat when they are victorious over the English. Comments like the famous statement made by the Chairman of the WRU, following a huge defeat by New Zealand – 'Well, I suppose now we just go back to beating England every year' – simply fuel the fire of antagonism.

In fact, Wales did not play well in this game. We were not very successful at getting over the gain line from set pieces, and we failed to recycle the ball quickly enough. Too often, we played the ball close to the tackle area and our attacks were snuffed out by the impressive English forwards. Knowing England's power up front, we should have varied the play by moving the ball wide or turning the defence through kicks. England had plenty of opportunities, but failed to convert points into pressure.

The Welsh players showed tremendous grit and determination, quite simply refusing to accept defeat as a possibility. They fought for every ball, and rebuffed wave after wave of English attacks. Everybody tackled ferociously and Jenkins kept putting over penalties to keep us in the hunt. If the English game is special to the Welsh supporters, it is also the big one for the players. Yet they refused to be wound up by the occasion. They had clearly learnt their lesson from the débâcle against Ireland, and kept their discipline in what was a thoroughly professional, dogged performance.

My feeling at half-time was that this simply was not going to be England's day. With minutes to go, England's arrogance cost them dear. They were awarded a kickable penalty in the dying minutes of the match. Had they taken the kick at goal they would, very probably, have gained a cushion of nine points, meaning that Wales would have to score twice to win the match. They would also have used up time. Instead, they chose to kick for position. Dallaglio then gave away a penalty, for a charge on Colin Charvis. Wales kicked for position, and from the resulting lineout Scott Gibbs produced his moment of magic. The instant he received the ball, just outside the English twenty-two, the hairs rose on the back of my neck and I knew something was on. The try was a classic. It must have been replayed on television as often as Gareth Edwards's great score for the Barbarians against New Zealand, and every time it is shown it's guaranteed to get Welshmen to their feet. We still had to depend on Jenkins for the conversion to secure a win, but all true supporters knew they could rely on him. I have never before seen a Welsh victory evoke such passion. English supporters, stiff upper lips clenched in defeat, were amazed as Welsh supporters ran through their repertoire of victory hymns, with tears in their eyes.

The Dragon Awakes

Although he played it down, I'm sure Graham was as thrilled as the rest of us by the England game. He summed up the match: 'We didn't play well, but this was a hugely emotional match and we can be rightly proud. We scrummaged well and our lineout was effective. In the end we won, courtesy of Neil Jenkins and a glorious run from Scott Gibbs. But the most pleasing aspect of the game was the determination that the team displayed. The players never lost their self-belief, and they kept their discipline and focus. The team spirit, the work rate and the desire to give an extra 20 per cent was awesome. At Wembley, we became a team! I was more pleased by this result than by the game in Paris, where we played with a lot of verve and fire but nearly lost it in the second half. Against England we were more disciplined and played with more control – even though the game wasn't going well, we hung in there. We came of age in that game, because although we were under a lot of pressure the guys refused to give in. We have come a long way in a short period, but there is still a huge mountain to climb. Working towards the World Cup we have to maintain and improve our standards and become consistent and competitive with the best teams in the world. However, the immediate challenge is a difficult tour to Argentina.' This attitude is typical of Henry. Whilst we supporters continued to luxuriate in the glow of success against England, Henry's mind was already focused on Argentina.

Having experienced the Five Nations tournament for the first time, Henry was also giving some thought to the way it is organised. He is no respecter of sacred cows. While he is adamant that the tournament is an amazing event, unequalled anywhere else in the rugby world, he is also conscious of its deficiencies. 'I would like to see the Six Nations matches played in a block, with no club rugby being played for the duration of the tournament. With the tournaments in New Zealand you keep the team together for the duration. This is obviously beneficial in terms of team-building. You have time to address

THE DRAGON AWAKES

the weakness exposed in games and correct them before the next match. With the Home Internationals, after each match the players go back to their clubs and the team is broken up for a week. It's very hard for the players to stay focused as they go back and forth between international and domestic rugby. It is also nerve-wracking as a coach to sit and watch your players involved in club rugby, anticipating that some of them could well be injured when you need them the following week.'

Henry is lobbying the powers-that-be to change the system. He wants the games to be played over an eight-week period, during which time there would be no club rugby, and the squad would remain together for the entire period. Hopefully, this system will be adopted in the near future. It has obvious advantages for the national squads and their coaches. It would also be beneficial for the clubs. The domestic season is fragmented by the intrusion of the Five Nations. If Graham Henry is worried that his players may pick up an injury between international matches, club coaches have the same worry about their players whilst on international duty. With league position determining entry into Europe, club coaches can ill afford to lose star players through knocks picked up playing for their country. Having thrown the idea into the pot, Henry got down to the business in hand and prepared for Argentina.

THREE

Putting The Roof On

THE 1999 HOME INTERNATIONAL SEASON drew to a close on a successful note. It had been a mixed season, with two wins and two defeats, plus the win against the Italians. Not perhaps a total transformation, but none the less a good beginning. The mood in the camp was very positive. After all, we had finished the season with three straight victories, two of them against the sides who are unquestionably the strongest in the Northern Hemisphere. In days of old this would have been the time for the players to play a bit of sevens or pack their boots away and relax for the summer months, but in the modern world the rugby circus seems to roll on all year round.

For the current crop of Welsh international players, the summer months promised a constant round of matches. First up was a tour of Argentina, and this was to be followed by summer matches against South Africa, Canada, France and the USA. After that there was the little matter of the Rugby World Cup! Many people wondered whether, given the gruelling schedule that lay ahead, the tour to Argentina was possibly surplus to requirements. This was obviously at the back of Graham's mind too, but he had no choice but to accept that the tour was in the IRB schedule and had to be used to the team's advantage.

The tour was probably undervalued by the Welsh rugby public. The vast majority of supporters see Argentina as a second division rugby nation, and a tour there never really captures the collective imagination. In reality, tours to Argentina are notoriously tough, and no Welsh team had ever won a Test series against the Argentinians on their home soil. Argentina play a very static, forward-oriented game, and even the regional sides offer a very physical and abrasive challenge. This certainly proved true on the tour. All the matches were tough, but Wales came through to win the series 2–0.

The tour was important on a number of counts. Firstly, by beating Argentina in their own country the team achieved something which even the great teams of the '70s had failed to do. This signalled to the players that they didn't have to live in the shadow of the previous golden era. It also helped to develop a winning habit. Wales had now won five games on the trot, a significant number. This was a winning run the like of which had not been seen for twenty years or more.

The tour also served to build team spirit amongst the players. On tour in an alien and even hostile environment, a team can go one of two ways. Either it fragments and divides under pressure, or it closes ranks and becomes stronger. In Argentina, the Welsh team spirit became stronger and so did their sense of self-belief. The aspect of the players returning from Argentina could not have been further removed from that of the shellshocked individuals who had returned from Pretoria a year earlier.

The treadmill ground on relentlessly; nine international matches in just over six months and still no respite for the small group of players chosen to represent Wales. Fortunately, we had won our last five Tests. Buoyed by their success, the players seemed to be wearing well. They all appeared remarkably fresh and upbeat as they prepared for their next test.

The Dragon Awakes

The match against South Africa, on 26 June 1999, gave the perfect opportunity to gauge how far Wales had come under Graham Henry's stewardship. It took place, significantly, a year to the day after that horrendous defeat in Pretoria. The Welsh team was very different to that understrength squad that had toured a year earlier. Only Dafydd James, Mark Taylor and Colin Charvis remained. The South African outfit had also changed. Some of the stars were out injured, and it was a very young South African team that became the first to run out on to the pitch at the new Millennium Stadium, but they were led out by the great Gary Teichmann, and they were still very much the world champions.

Any game against the giants of the Southern Hemisphere is always immense, but today the occasion was heightened by the fact that this was also to be the opening of the new stadium. Coming into Cardiff, the new building dominated the skyline. Close up it was even more impressive, like a vast spaceship looming over the town centre, a symbol of the all-pervading importance of the game closest to Welsh hearts. There was a carnival atmosphere in Cardiff on the day of the match and the air of anticipation was palpable, despite the fact that the stadium would be only one-third full. The streets were crowded with supporters hoping to pick up a ticket for the first match in the newly rebuilt home of Welsh rugby.

Inside the stadium, even its severest critics had to admit that they had been wrong. Ever since the idea of a new ground had been raised, it had served as yet another topic for wrangling over in the insular world of Welsh rugby. Many had seen it as a white elephant, a vainglorious monument to the egos that run the game in Wales. The Cardiff Arms Park was good enough for us and besides, it was the repository of so many memories. To us, the Arms Park was the citadel that represented the home of rugby. At a time when all our efforts should be concentrated on improving the game in Wales, the WRU was more interested in creating a showpiece. Now its critics were proved wrong. Much as we had all loved the Arms Park this was magnificent, a truly awesome stadium.

With only 27,000 people in the ground and many of the stands still bare of seats, there was a danger that the occasion could have been an anticlimax. There were teething troubles: the computerised turnstiles didn't work, and where I sat the rain poured from the unfinished roof and ran in torrents down the terracing, but even the harshest critic couldn't fail to be impressed by the imposing surroundings. It must have been particularly pleasing for Glanmor Griffiths, Chairman of the WRU, to be so fully vindicated in his decision to press for the building of a new home for Welsh rugby.

The fact that half the ground was still a building site didn't seem to matter, as the crowd of 27,000 turned the half-finished stadium into a cauldron of emotion. I have always been a big fan of the old North Enclosure; in the days before stadiums were all-seater, the North Enclosure had seemed to me to be the heart of Welsh rugby, a surging ruck of ten thousand highly vocal supporters. The atmosphere in the new ground matched anything I had experienced in that bear pit, and it had the advantage that you also had a view – you could actually see the match. I was seated five rows from the back, a similar position to the one I had occupied during our last match, against England at the old Arms Park. There you had felt distant from the action; here you seemed to be on top of the pitch.

In the build-up to the game Graham had been very low-key. This was 'a game too far', he had told the press. The Welsh fans should not expect too much, the players were tired, and the chances of victory were remote. But we were getting wise to the ways of our new coach, and we took what he said with a huge pinch of salt. This was judgement day for Henry's Welsh team. They had beaten France with style and panache and sneaked home against England with gritty determination, but we had

The Dragon Awakes

beaten those sides before. No Welsh side had ever won against South Africa, but after coming close against them the previous autumn, today we thought we might finally better the world champions.

There were the usual formalities as various local dignitaries enjoyed having a bit of time in the public eye, making speeches praising both the new ground and themselves for having such vision. However, most of the crowd was probably paying more attention to the antics of the Ginger Monster. This kilted Welshman, with a huge ginger wig and comic false ears, has become something of an institution at Welsh games over the past few years. He runs on to score a try using a toy sheep as a ball, and he then converts his try with an excellent impersonation of Neil Jenkins's kicking style.

Eventually the speeches were over and the Ginger Monster had entertained the crowd by scoring the first try at the new stadium. Then the real Neil Jenkins got the game under way. Wales took the game to the South Africans, and completely dominated the first half. Importantly, we disrupted the scrum, which is the key to the South African side. South African rugby relies heavily on its macho image, and it is crucial for them to physically dominate the opposition. The chief architect of this destruction was Peter Rogers who had his opposition prop, Cobus Visagie, tied in knots after the first couple of scrums.

The Welsh lineout worked smoothly, due to the superb work of Chris Wyatt, who turns even the worst throw into good clean possession. On the back of this excellent possession Scott Quinnell was at his rampaging best, consistently getting over the gain line and punching holes in the South African defence. Howley and Jenkins controlled the game well, and South Africa simply never got a look in. Welsh dominance was rewarded with a string of penalties, duly converted by Jenkins. The crowning moment of the half came after about twenty-five minutes. Ironically, the score came from one of the rare occasions when the Welsh lineout failed to work. Wyatt couldn't get to a poor throw-in from Garin Jenkins, and South Africa took the ball only to lose it again to Charvis at the tail of the line. Charvis fed Howley and the ball went down the line to Taylor, who handed off his opposite number and ran in from twenty yards. Despite their elation, Wales got straight back to business and continued their siege of the South African line. The continued pressure brought no further score, and Wales went into half-time leading 19–6.

Presumably there were some harsh words in the visitors' dressing-room at half-time, and South Africa started the second half with greater aggression and determination. There were some fraught moments as the South Africans camped out on our try-line, but the Welsh defence was immense. There were try-saving tackles from Jenkins and Allan Bateman, and Mike Voyle saved a try by getting under the ball to prevent South Africa grounding it. For me, as an old wing forward, the hero of the half was Brett Sinkinson. He was awesome, making hit after hit, invariably turning his man and driving him back. On the day, he was comparable to the great Josh Kronfeld.

A South African score was inevitable, and after what seemed like hours of relentless pressure Swanepoel eventually pulled back a try for the visiting team. A penalty from Du Toit brought the score to 19–14, and thoughts of the Wembley disappointment crept into the minds of the Welsh support. Fortunately, the players were more resolute and on one of our brief forays into the opposition half, Scott Quinnell smashed through the South African defence. Quick ball from the ensuing ruck was moved out to Gareth Thomas, who scored in the corner. Jenkins converted, and then put over another penalty. With the score at 29–14, we were out of sight at last. Montgomery scored a consolation try to pull it back to 29–19, but the game was won.

When the whistle went elation was tinged with relief. South

THE DRAGON AWAKES

Africa had thrown everything at us in the second half and Wales had needed all their reserves of energy and resolve to withstand the onslaught. This was truly a momentous day. We had proclaimed the fact that we had one of the finest grounds in world rugby, and then shown that we had a team worthy of gracing the new citadel.

The result showed that the Welsh team had come a long way in the last twelve months, and the manner of the win said a lot about the new-found professionalism of the squad. In attack they had been focused and patient, keeping possession and waiting for the gaps to appear. In defence they had been disciplined and dedicated. Graham told me afterwards that the team had made over eighty tackles in the second half of the game. That number is usually made throughout an entire match, but we had made it in one half. Despite the pressure, we didn't give away any unnecessary penalties. At times of crisis the self-belief, born out of five successive victories, and the team spirit, forged in Argentina, had enabled Wales to battle through.

The transformation, so it seemed, was complete. The ragged, deflated team who had returned from South Africa twelve months earlier was now a focused, disciplined unit, capable of beating the best in the world. Nowhere was the transformation more obvious than in the form of our outside-half. Neil Jenkins has always been something of a whipping boy for the majority of Welsh fans. OK, he's a great place-kicker, a points machine, but he doesn't satisfy the nation's desire for a jinking magical outside-half in the mould of Cliff Morgan or Phil Bennett. Against South Africa Jenkins silenced his critics, running the game efficiently from outside-half. His distribution was excellent and his kicking from the hand was superb. In addition, he contributed nineteen points with the boot. Suddenly, he was a hero.

The Welsh fans and the media are extremely fickle. All the criticism heaped on Jenkins in the past was now forgotten. Wales were world-beaters. The win over South Africa showed that the results against France and England were not just flukes – the Welsh team had really progressed. They were consistently putting in top-class performances, and had shown that they had the potential to upset even the best teams. On this showing, even Australia and the mighty All Blacks might not prove too much for us. Graham Henry had achieved so much in less than a year; surely he could push the team further still in the next three months? If he could, the Rugby World Cup was a distinct possibility, and Graham Henry could do no wrong.

Graham himself was more circumspect. Yes, he was very impressed with the team's performance, and although he played it down, he was extremely proud of them. In many ways this was the most complete performance of his tenure. The defence had been truly magnificent, and the team had shown the kind of professionalism that he demanded from them. At the same time, he was wary of the overreaction of the Welsh fans and the media. The game against South Africa was the peak of his achievements since taking charge, but it was a one-off event. The circumstances of the day were unique. The return to Cardiff and the collective desire to make up for the recent defeats at the hands of South Africa had raised the team to a new level, but the big question was whether Wales could sustain that level of performance over a number of games.

Graham Henry would not be convinced by only one such display. The Welsh lineout had worked well for much of the match, but it remained a worry for Wales. Chris Wyatt had contributed a great deal, but it was asking a lot to expect him to be our sole ball-winner in that department. Another worry was the lack of strength in depth. The players on the field had done a great job, but in the event of injuries, were there players waiting in the wings to replace the heroes of 26 June? Despite the historic win, Graham Henry was aware that his team was still some way from a position where they could realistically expect to lift the World Cup in four months' time.

FOUR

The Build-up Begins

THE GAME AGAINST SOUTH AFRICA had been a celebration of the team's return to Wales after their exile in Wembley. It was also part of a schedule of matches that had to be played in order to satisfy legal requirements concerning public safety. Graham Henry had suggested it was a match too far, and that the players needed some rest. However, with the World Cup looming there was no time for the players to rest. Henry had been contracted by the WRU until the World Cup of 2003, and at the time of his appointment the general consensus was that his aim should be to produce a competitive team in time for that tournament. However, the recent run of success meant that people were beginning to feel that he might even achieve this in time for the World Cup in Wales, and the expectation around the country was building.

The players were given one month off before reassembling for a series of training camps building up to the event in October. There were three friendly internationals planned, which would give Graham the opportunity to fine-tune his team and would also satisfy the health and safety regulations concerning the new stadium. Given that they had been playing continuously for almost nine months, the players were remarkably fresh when they gathered in Brecon in late July for the first of these training sessions. The media circus was also starting to roll, and the squad was followed around the country by teams of journalists and camera crews.

The first session, lasting four days, was held at Christ College, Brecon. Fortunately the weather was kind, and the squad trained in the sun on the manicured grounds of the public school, in front of the dramatic backdrop of the Brecon Beacons. I joined the squad for these sessions, and on the first day I got my first real taste of the kind of public scrutiny the players were constantly under, for, in addition to the media, hundreds of spectators turned up to watch them train.

In public relations terms, the players are a dream. After two hours of working out in the baking sun, they will take the time to sign autographs and chat to the children who have come along to see their heroes, something that can take at least another hour. These may be top-flight, international sports stars, but they are still close enough to their roots to appreciate the feelings of the fans. Shane Howarth, one of the most sought-after players in the country, is always amongst the last to leave any signing session. 'I don't like to leave until I've signed for every kid that wants my autograph,' he told me. 'Once, when I was a kid, I asked a famous All Black second row for his autograph and he told me to fuck off. I was gutted to be treated like that by a man I worshipped. I always remember that feeling, and I figure it's my duty not to let those kids down.'

But by the time Graham Henry's rugby circus had finished its tour around Wales, the demands being made on the team were too great even for Howarth to manage. In Pembroke they were besieged by hundreds of fans and eventually had to drive off leaving some of them disappointed. 'It was awful,' said Howarth. 'You could see all these faces, kids holding out pictures to be signed, and we just couldn't do it. I said we should stop the bus and go back, but we would never have got away.'

The continuing freshness of the team was due in part to their recent success. They were on a six-match winning run and the entire nation was behind them, a fact which was demonstrated everywhere they went. The other factor was the training regime of fitness coach Steve Black. It was during these training camps that I first became aware of the importance of Blackie to the squad. He is just such a great bloke. The players all love him, and evidently want to do well for him. He is also always incredibly upbeat; he enjoys every minute of what he does and his enthusiasm is infectious.

It is impossible to be around Blackie and not be fired up by his passion and zest. His training methods are unique. Graham Henry explained to me that that was partly what attracted him to Blackie in the first place: 'He's a one-off,' he told me. 'No disrespect, but there are a lot of clones in the fitness game. Blackie introduces the unexpected and keeps the players thinking all the time. He works on their minds as well as their bodies.' The freshness of Black's approach became apparent in those first few days at Brecon. The players went through hours of training drills out on the playing fields of Christ College, and at no time did I see them working with a ball. 'The boys have been on a treadmill for the past nine months,' he explained. 'When you do that there is nothing left in the tank, and the game stops being fun. I want them hungry again. I want them itching to get their hands on a rugby ball.' During their stay in the mountains the team played basketball and water polo, and Blackie even arranged a visit to a dance studio. But no rugby.

After their week in Brecon, the squad returned to Cardiff where they trained at the David Lloyd Tennis Centre, making great use of the weights room. I suspect any regular gym posers made themselves pretty scarce when they realised they were competing with the likes of Craig Quinnell. Watching them

THE DRAGON AWAKES

work out in the gym really brings home the power of these guys – even backs like Ebbw Vale scrum-half Dai Llewellyn were lifting scary amounts of metal. When they weren't heaving massive weights, the players enjoyed relaxing, lighthearted games of tennis and squash. It was reassuring for me to see that even these guys have weak points and while I wouldn't want to meet them on the rugby field, there are a few I would take on on the squash court! Even in these friendly games, the competitive nature of these top sportsmen was apparent. Shane Howarth is someone who would try his hardest to win if he were playing tiddlywinks!

At this time, I also began to see the importance of other members of the management team. Even though they hadn't played a match for a month, there was a constantly changing injury list; players with niggling problems, picked up over the past nine months. Mark Davies, ex-Wales and Swansea wing forward and known to the team as Carcass, had a steady stream of visitors to his treatment bench. Graham had also brought in Mike Wadsworth, a Cardiff masseur, who was in great demand easing out tired muscles.

The real work of the week, however, was in speed training. The players were put through a series of sprint drills by Steve Black. 'This week,' said Blackie, 'we are paying homage to speed. We use short periods of intense activity, with rest periods in between. For the next few weeks we will be doing a lot of reaction work, making sure that they get into the habit of being fast and that they fulfil their potential for speed.' Black feels that many people involved with fitness training for professional rugby have misinterpreted fitness, reiterating his earlier point that: 'Too often they went for endurance, for general fitness. To compete at the top level in international sport, the key is speed.' Blackie's theory about the habit of speed made me think back to a conversation I'd had with Graham earlier in the year. He had referred to what he called the plod factor: on his arrival in Wales, he had been struck by the slowness of many of the players. He was not talking about their speed as sprinters, but about their general movements. They had not yet developed the habit of speed in their everyday lives.

As the World Cup approached, the coaching regime was based on fine-tuning both skills and fitness. Looking forward, with only two months to go before the launch of the Rugby World Cup, Black was adamant that the team still had some hard graft to put in in preparation for the tournament: 'In fitness terms,' he told me, 'we are 80 per cent along the way to where we want to be, but the last 20 per cent is the hardest. That first 80 per cent is relatively easy to get. It's like when you build a house. Putting up the shell of the building is three-quarters of the job, but it's getting all the fixtures and fittings in place that takes time. That's where we are today, putting in the finishing touches. If we can get that extra percentage by the time we get to the World Cup, then we will be competitive. That doesn't mean we will win, but it does mean that we'll give other teams a hard time. If we are on the edge we will be competitive: if we meet other teams who are also on the edge then they will probably beat us, but we will compete. Of course the games are all one-offs and on the day either team can win, but in rugby, much more than in soccer, the better team tends to win. You don't get as many upsets in rugby.'

Blackie's enthusiasm and upbeat attitude seemed to have spread to the players. After the disastrous tour to South Africa, most supporters would probably have expected there to be an air of desperation in the camp but Steve insisted that there has been a positive attitude in the camp since day one: 'It's not so surprising. Whenever you join a new sporting team, the players always want to impress the new manager or coach – it's the new broom syndrome – and the boys here have always been positive. It's just a case of how long the new work ethic lasts. If I can go back to soccer, how many times do you see a team struggling until they bring in a new manager and win their next two or three games, only to slip back into their losing ways? The key thing with this Welsh team is that we had those initial results, but we haven't slipped back; instead, we've built on it. There is now some longevity to our success; we have achieved some stability, created an environment which allows the players' talent to flourish, and now they have to take advantage of that.'

Although Black was happy with the progress that had been made during the last twelve months, he felt that the team was in no way the finished article. 'This team will be better in four years' time, but the improvement over the next few years will not be as marked as during this initial period. The results have been fantastic, even the bad results have a positive aspect to them. Don't get me wrong, I love winning. I'm a terrible, horrible, awful loser. I'm not into good sportsmanship, I wish I were and I tell my children that they should be sporting and accept defeat, but I'm an awful loser, me. But defeat is not so bad if you learn something on the way, if you look at why you lost and determine that it will not happen again. You might lose again, but not for the same reason as the last time. What we are promoting at present is the habit of winning and the players are starting to believe in themselves. They refuse to yield. You could see that in the South African game – the boys refused to be beat. It's a factor with all the best teams, we had it at Newcastle Falcons and you see it now with Manchester United. They refuse to yield.'

The three friendlies played prior to the World Cup tested Graham Henry's meticulous preparation methods. He employs ex-international forward Alun Carter to prepare videos on all of his opponents, and watches these to seek out weak points in the opposition. The process is time-consuming, but beneficial. Carter prepares a record of each team, focusing on key areas such as the scrum, the lineout and kick-offs over eight or more matches, and from this Henry can form an impression of the pattern of play employed by each team. Normally he watches these videos the week prior to a match, but with Wales playing three matches in ten days he was kept very busy.

The players also had videos to watch: Carter made a video profile of each individual, and Henry made assessments of their strengths and weaknesses. These were to be used by the squad members to help them develop their game over the coming months. The team could watch these videos at any time, and the idea was that Graham would sit down with each player and go over the video report to see what progress had been made.

As the game against Canada drew closer, the intensity of training picked up for the players. Much of the training in the preceding weeks had not involved a ball, and the team were raring for a game. Their level of enthusiasm was remarkable, considering the treadmill they had all been on for the past year.

In the build-up to the World Cup the squad was housed at the Copthorne Hotel, on the outskirts of Cardiff. Their surroundings may have been very comfortable, but living in a hotel brought other pressures and concerns for the management team. For a start, the players were living in a very public environment and were unable to get much privacy. But the biggest danger was boredom. Effectively the squad were on tour, but without the release that matches bring. None of them had played any competitive rugby since the Test against South Africa, and although they were now raring for action, Graham expected there to be some rustiness in the game against Canada.

To minimise the effect of this lack of pre-match practice, Henry started to make training sessions more physical and began to include a lot of contact work, not usual in training prior to a match. The weather prior to the games was appalling and much of the training had to be done indoors, at the Equestrian Centre at Pencoed. Graham described that week's routine: 'This is our first Test match for ten weeks and during that time the players haven't done any contact work. To get them into the groove, we started with a heavy scrummaging session on Monday, followed by a lot of attack stuff, getting the ball out wide.

'On the Tuesday we did a lot of defence work, making tackles and turning the ball over. We had a lot of mini-games, seven v seven, concentrating on the tackle area and defence around ruck and maul. A common error with coaches is that they do a lot of work on lineouts and scrums, and less on the tackle area. In an average international there will be something like eighteen scrums, twenty-six lineouts and over ninety tackles. The tackle area is where it all happens and where games are lost and won.

'On Thursday we did a lot of teamwork, looking at set pieces and working on our game plan. Even this session was opposed, which is unusual so close to a Test, but we were rusty and the guys needed it. We have put them under a lot of pressure this week, but they have to be exposed to that. There's no point talking about rustiness after Saturday.'

Henry's rigorous preparation methods were stifled by the fact that he could only get hold of one video of the current Canadian team in action, but he knew what sort of match to expect. 'Canada will be strong at scrum and lineout and around the fringes. We've got to stretch them. They are hard, physical men who play with a lot of fire, and we will have to respect them. They will play a forward-oriented, stationary game – in other words, the old UK game. We want to play at speed, without too many stoppages, and must put several phases together. They will find that hard to handle, because they're not used to that sort of game. We must play for field position early on, because we don't want to put ourselves under pressure. If that happens, if we play it down our end, we could find ourselves in trouble. I've told the players to set some targets so we're not running round like headless chucks.

'We need to get the forwards in the game early and switch the play from the set pieces, to move their forwards around. What I have learnt about the Canadians is that they tend to congregate around the tackle area instead of spreading the defence. As the game progresses, hopefully we can achieve some dominance and then take the game out wider, but this can be dangerous: the wider you take the game the more vulnerable you are. That's the trouble with the game today. You can turn the ball over very easily out wide, if you don't have enough support, and then you're in the shit. So if it goes out to the winger the centres have got to go in and secure the ball. The winger often gets the blame for hanging on to the ball, but if he releases quickly there is a danger it can get turned over. If we are going to play to our potential, we have got to expand the game and get the ball out wider as the game goes on, but this must be balanced.'

On the Friday the players went through a light session at the stadium. This was really just to keep them loose, and give them a feel for the ground. The stadium looked fantastic, but was still crawling with workmen. The capacity for the Canada game had been set at 55,000, and the team were anticipating a fervent atmosphere. The stadium was about 80 per cent complete, a condition which Graham equated with the state of the team. On the day of the match Graham gave his team talk at the hotel before the players departed for the stadium. Once there they became Blackie's concern, and he set about building them up psychologically.

Even at this point, it is possible for Graham to make slight alterations to the game plan. On one occasion while at Auckland, he decided on the morning of the match to put Jonah Lomu into the lineout. This was designed to get the opposition thinking, and it worked. While the other team was watching Jonah, Auckland scored in the other corner. That stunt typifies Henry's approach to the game. His philosophy could be summed up as 'make it happen' and his method is one of empowerment. He realises that whatever he does on the training field, whatever he says in the changing-room, only the players can really run the game on the park, so he wants them to be bold and decisive. To this end he encourages a number of senior players to become involved in the decision-making process both on and off the field. On the night before an international there is always a captain's meeting. Henry has no input in this, normally he just looks in on the meeting and says nothing. It is an opportunity for all of the players to have their say on the game, and for the captain to restate the game plan as he sees it.

I was able to listen in on his team talk before the Canada game, and it gives a real insight into the way that he approaches the job. His delivery was calm and measured; he left the passion-building exercise to Steve Black. Despite his understated delivery, the players hung on his every word in reverential silence. Henry started his talk by stressing that this match was another opportunity to build on recent successes, and he catalogued these: 'We've taken lots of opportunities this year. The French result, first time in twenty-four years in Paris, the Argentina tour, the first time a Welsh side has won a series in a major overseas tour, the first time we've beaten South Africa in ninety-three years. We've a chance of winning seven in a row – the first time since the 1970s, with the great team of that time that you know more about than I do.

'Because it's the first time in twenty-four years that we've had this chance, it means it's bloody difficult. It's got to be difficult; otherwise it would be done all the time. Outside our little nation, look at South Africa, last year, going for eighteen wins against England. They couldn't do it. Since then they have played seven Test matches, and only won three. The All Blacks lost five in a row last year, the worst run ever by a New Zealand team. European teams: only one team has won a match since the Five Nations, France against Samoa. No other European side, apart from us, has won. What I'm trying to say is, it's not bloody easy, guys.

'We have to decide; where is this team going? Has it got the ability, the character, and the endurance to go on from here? At the back of my mind I wonder whether you're wallowing in self-satisfaction. You've created some special moments in winning six in a row – maybe that's enough for you. Maybe mediocrity, the average, is OK. Do you want it enough? Today we're at the crossroads. Do you have what it takes to go on from here and be the best? If you start paying too much attention to the record, to the numbers, then you're in trouble. It's the process that matters, what you do out there, as individuals, that matters. And it's what you do out there as a team that matters.

'Nothing will annoy me more than people not expressing themselves and being bold, and showing their ability. I don't give a stuff if you make mistakes, as long as you go out there and play. *Everybody plays, right!* That's what we're about. You express yourselves, you let it all hang out, and you get outside the square. You take them on, you're bold, 'cos that's what winning is about. If you get timid and scared and you start worrying about the result, you're down the dunny. Let's have some enjoyment out there; express yourselves. Be the top footballers on the field that you've got the ability to be.

'That's the crossroads we're at now. We've created something that's very special, and the only way we can go on from here is if you get outside yourself. That's what we're going to do today. You play with huge endeavour, boldness and excitement and you do the business. OK. It starts with accuracy and stability up front. Quick pace intensity. You hit and it's gone. It means every bugger working his arse off. Get on the shoulder of the ball carrier. It's about huge defence. Knock 'em back in the tackle. It's about defence at first phase. If you get it right at first phase, you don't have to worry about second phase 'cos they're going backwards. It's also about discipline. Remember the dark ages? I do. Ireland, Scotland, we were a childish bunch of rugby players. Now we do the business, and we keep our cool. But most of all – express yourselves.'

The speech was delivered in perfectly measured tones, and the intensity, the volume and the passion ebbed and flowed as he underlined the key points and exhorted the players to 'get outside of themselves and be bold'. I don't know if Graham has ever studied rhetoric, I think he's just a natural orator, but he could certainly teach a few politicians a thing or two about the art of public speaking. His ability is probably a direct result of all those years as a school teacher. He is at ease talking to a group of thirty people, be they schoolchildren or international rugby players.

As I said, a coach's power stops once the players get on the field. Then it's down to them. Despite Graham's carefully orchestrated training regime, despite his powerful team talk, the players didn't do the business that afternoon. They won comfortably, 33–19, but it was a performance lacking boldness and incisiveness. The result was never in doubt, but it was a stop-start affair, with very little fluidity and far too many mistakes. Canada fought hard and did all they could to frustrate Wales's attempts to play a flowing game. Gareth Rees kicked superbly to keep Canada in the game, and the Canadians must have been pleased with their performance.

Wales showed some good touches, but the rustiness which Graham had mentioned was very evident. However, as the match wore on Wales improved and in the last twenty minutes they started to play in the manner expected of them. After the game Graham was typically forthright. No excuses, simply: 'We didn't play very well.' The game had served its purpose. It had blown away a few cobwebs and, besides, it was another victory.

Now the Welsh team was really on the treadmill. There was no time for rest. Canada were history, and the players had to prepare for a tougher test in a week's time, against France. The week began with more video viewing. The match against Canada was reviewed and lessons were learnt from the performance. Graham watched the tapes with the players and pointed out the high and low points. On his own he watched tapes of French

The Dragon Awakes

games, looking for weak links and familiarising himself with their plays. It was important that Wales stepped up a gear against the French, firstly because they are stronger opponents than the Canadians, but also because back-to-back wins over the French would be seen as another milestone in the development of the Welsh team.

The training sessions were less physical than they had been the previous week. Players needed time to recuperate, and the sessions were designed to ensure that they would start with a 'full tank' against the French.

At the same time as the players worked ceaselessly in their training camp, the media circus was gaining intensity as we moved towards the World Cup. Newspapers and television ran daily updates on the build-up to the competition, and the players were constantly being asked for interviews and comment on developments within the camp. Graham gave the media plenty of copy during this time. His decision to use Allan Bateman, a world-class centre, on the wing, sparked one debate. Bateman, we were told, was unhappy at being forced to play out of position. There may have been an element of truth in this. No player wants to play out of position and Allan is certainly no lover of the position of wing. He summed up his feelings by declaring, 'I've had a long-standing loathing of playing on the wing since my days at Maesteg.' But his desire to play for Wales, plus his consummate professionalism, meant he would never have broken ranks over the issue.

Another thorny issue was the drafting in of more overseas players. Henry had often commented on the lack of strength in depth in certain positions in Wales. It was announced that Jason Jones-Hughes, a young Australian centre of Welsh ancestry, had expressed a desire to be considered for selection for Wales, the land of his fathers. The Australian Rugby Union had put a block on the move, and while this situation was being settled Henry brought in Andy Marinos from South Africa. Wales's two Welsh

The Dragon Awakes

Kiwis, Brett Sinkinson and Shane Howarth, were now firmly established in the Welsh team, but some commentators took issue with the need for more 'foreign' players joining the Welsh ranks. One leading sports writer questioned Graham on the need for more imports. 'Surely,' he asked, 'there is home-grown talent that could be used rather than importing players from South Africa or Australia?' 'Name them,' was Graham's reply. There was some hilarity amongst the gathered ranks of pressmen as their red-faced colleague was pressed for the name of a Welsh-born centre who could fill the place of Marinos and Jones-Hughes.

While the press debated the merits of Marinos's inclusion in the squad, the team accepted him readily and got on with the task in hand: defeating the French. Before the game the French asked that the game should be treated as a trial match, and that they should be allowed to use their entire squad. Permission was refused and there was some confusion on the day as the French made questionable substitutions, which resulted in delays as the match adjudicator enforced the letter of the law. Wales fielded what was, arguably, their strongest side, and won in a physical, often bad-tempered contest.

Although 34–23 was a convincing score, there was still evidence of rustiness amongst the players. The quality of play and the boldness that Graham demanded was apparent in some passages of play, but the game didn't match up to the spectacle that had taken place in Paris six months earlier. Still, a win is a win, and Wales had now extended their winning run to eight games.

As a build-up to the World Cup, the two games against Canada and France seemed well balanced. Canada had offered a powerful, physical challenge, and France were a proven force in world rugby. England, in their preparations, had opted for easier run-outs against less powerful opposition. This offered them the opportunity to fine-tune their team on the field, while not putting them under too much pressure. Which approach would prove the most successful? Only time would tell.

THE DRAGON AWAKES

There were positives and negatives to be taken from the Welsh matches. The front five were very strong, and could realistically hold their ground against the world's best, but our lineout was exposed as being somewhat limited. Chris Wyatt was outstanding, but he remained our only realistic option. Craig Quinnell's awesome power was needed in the loose, but the lineout is not really his forte. In the backs there still didn't seem to be room for Allan Bateman. The experiment of playing him on the wing had proved inconclusive, and yet it seemed criminal not to make use of his obvious class and skill. On the wing we lacked out-and-out pace, and there was really no cover for Shane Howarth at full-back.

Reconciling these issues was not something even Graham Henry could achieve in the next month, and so fine-tuning the present team was his aim in that period of time. The squad consisted of thirty-plus players, and the second string were given a run-out, two days after the French match, against the USA. Henry continued the experiment of playing Bateman on the wing, and despite his disdain for the position, Bateman reacted by scoring three tries. Not bad, for a guy playing out of position. Wales won easily, 53–24, and the players had a few days at home before travelling to North Wales for another training camp. This camp, and a second one held in Pembrokeshire, were dedicated to more fine-tuning, but they carried the usual burden of media and public attention. In the search for some privacy, Graham took the squad off to Portugal for a final squad session.

FIVE

SOME TIME IN THE SUN

GRAHAM HAD INVITED ME TO JOIN THE SQUAD for the trip to Portugal and so, on Thursday, 16 September, I joined the players at the Copthorne Hotel en route to Gatwick Airport. As we milled around in the foyer of the hotel, I noticed a face which seemed vaguely familiar. A young man, in Welsh training kit, sat near the entrance looking slightly nervous and awe-struck. Then I placed him. It was Rhys Williams, full-back for the Welsh Under-21 team. David Pickering explained to me that Rhys had been invited along for the ride, to gain some experience of life at the top. I was struck by the way the senior players went out of their way to make him feel at home.

Later, Rhys told me that it was slightly overwhelming to suddenly find himself amongst the players he had watched as a fan only a season ago. When he was a kid at school many of these players, such as Scott Quinnell and Allan Bateman, had been his heroes, and here he was preparing to play alongside them. This was Rhys's first taste of senior international rugby and he adjusted to it instantly, not only on the field, but off it as well. He handled the media's interest in him like a seasoned pro. It was obvious watching him on the training field that here was a star of the future.

The Dragon Awakes

In the press session before we left the Copthorne, Graham and Rob Howley made it clear that the team were heading off for four days of intensive training. This was definitely not an opportunity for a late holiday. After much hanging around for interviews and autograph signing we boarded the coach heading for Gatwick, and some time in the sun. The players had been living out of suitcases for most of the summer, and on the coach they rapidly fell into tour mode. Shane Howarth promptly shut himself off and whiled away the journey listening to music. The table at the back of the bus was commandeered by the card school. Lesson number one: don't play cards against Neil Boobyer! Garin Jenkins sat at the back of the bus talking, with childlike enthusiasm, about his latest discovery: the Internet. Others slept or read their way to Gatwick.

At the hotel it was a quick meal followed by a visit to the cinema for some players, while the management sat in the bar and worked over the final details in preparation for the next few days. The sobriety of the squad was illustrated by the fact that one player actually came over to ask Graham whether he was allowed a beer. Then everyone had an early night before the early flight to Portugal.

In Portugal, we were staying at Barringtons, a leisure complex half an hour from Faro Airport. Our stay there centred on the weights room and the training field, with recovery and relaxation time spent around the pool. Any time off was spent on the driving range, the putting green, the golf course or the snooker table. Lesson two: don't play snooker against Stephen Jones or Neil Jenkins. The squad trained three times a day, and the sessions were all extremely intensive and focused. The morning sessions were the most physical. One morning the session might involve heavy scrummaging and fitness routines, and on another the emphasis might be on defence, with opposed drills.

Any hopes that Graham had about these sessions taking place away from the glare of public scrutiny were soon shattered because after we had been there one day, Welsh expats and holidaymakers started to appear at the training sessions. Over the first two days a stream of journalists and camera crews also appeared, setting up camp on the steps outside the main building. The visiting holidaymakers were soon enlisted to the cause, and found themselves supplying extra weight on the scrummage machine. Those people gained first-hand experience of the intensity of the training as they were shunted around the playing fields by the Welsh pack. The tackle and defence sessions were equally physical and many spectators were left wincing at the impact of hefty Welshmen on tackle bag or contact pad. Even in training these guys do not give an inch, and tempers flared on more than one occasion.

The afternoon and evening sessions tended to concentrate more on set-piece moves, such as receiving kick-offs or plays from scrum and lineout. The players were shepherded through these periods by Graham, Blackie, Lynn Howells and David Pickering. All the periods of activity were relatively brief but intense, and players were kept alert by the constant changes thrown in by the coaches.

When the organised sessions were over some players would depart for a recovery period in the pool, while others would visit Carcass and masseur Mike Wadsworth for treatment for various niggles, old and new. What was striking was the number of players who stayed on the field after training in order to practise individual skills. It was the norm to see Jenks and Stephen Jones practising their kicking, while Shane Howarth fielded the kicks and returned the balls. Meanwhile Garin Jenkins and a couple of forwards would be practising lineouts. This was also the time when other players headed for the gym to lift a few weights.

The evenings were an illustration of how much things have changed in the era of professionalism. Any visiting journalists looking for stories of binge drinking and the nightly excesses normally associated with touring rugby players were sadly

The Dragon Awakes

disappointed. On three of the five nights the players sat around drinking hot chocolate and watching rugby league on Sky, with the benefit of expert analysis from Scott Quinnell and Allan Bateman. We had two nights out, but these were sober affairs. The first was a revelation. The energy the guys were expending on the training field had to be replaced, and the restaurant we visited on the second night had no idea what they were letting themselves in for in offering to cater for thirty rugby players. The meal took ages, as the players literally ate everything on the menu. One waiter looked thoroughly bemused as he tried to explain to Ben Evans that Beef Wellington is for two, only to be told that the huge dish would do nicely to follow the lobster he had ordered as a starter.

What rapidly became apparent was just how tight the players were as a unit. They had been living in each other's pockets for the last nine months, and theirs was very much a closed world. While they were polite and friendly to anyone outside the group, they kept their distance. Despite this the new arrivals in the squad were very quickly integrated into the unit, both on the field and off it. It was a huge change for Rhys Williams, but at least he was familiar with the culture.

Rhys was not the only new face on the tour. The conflict over Jason Jones-Hughes had finally been resolved and he joined the squad for the trip. Jason had the additional challenge of having to adapt to living in a foreign culture. He looked a trifle bemused by much of the banter, and spent a lot of his free time buried in a book. However, he told me that the players had been superb in helping him to settle in: 'When everybody went home for a few days before coming out here, I had to stay in the Copthorne. A lot of the boys rang me regularly to make sure I was alright and see if they could do anything for me.'

Jones-Hughes is a quietly spoken young man, who seemed to have taken the events of the last few months in his stride. 'I guess I'm still on a bit of a high. After all the waiting for clearance to play for Wales, everything suddenly happened very quickly,' he explained as we sat in the lounge at Barringtons. 'I'm getting a lot of new experiences and it's a lot to take in. The whole rugby culture here is immense compared to back in Australia. Over there it's a minority sport, whereas in Wales it's number one. It's great.'

Jason had to adapt not only to the change in lifestyle, but also to making adjustments to his game. 'It takes time to get used to other people's style of play, but I am familiarising myself with all the lines of running and patterns of play,' he said. 'It's a lot to take in, but the others have really helped. That is one of the outstanding things about the team – no bickering or cliquishness. Everybody is working for each other.' Jones-Hughes looked pretty sharp on the training field, and he was confident that he would have adapted to the Welsh style of play by the time October the First came around. After the World Cup he was looking forward to settling into life in Wales and, despite my best efforts to talk him into joining Ebbw Vale, playing for Newport.

Both Jason Jones-Hughes and I had been impressed by the professionalism in the Welsh camp. I wondered how different the preparations under Graham Henry had been from those for previous World Cups. One evening I had the chance to discuss the matter with Gareth Thomas. Alfie, as he is known to the squad, had been on the fringes of the Welsh team prior to the 1995 competition, held in South Africa. Four years on, he is an integral part of Graham Henry's squad. 'There's a real buzz about this squad,' he told me. 'There's a feeling that we can really achieve something as a team. Of course, the whole set-up is more professional now. In 1995 we were all amateurs, and it wasn't possible to devote a huge amount of time to preparation; I think we only had one weekend in Cardiff in which to prepare. We did a bit of team-building, but all the real work had to be done when we arrived in South Africa, and even then it was totally different to the way it is today. Now our training is very focused, while back in '95 it was a lot less scientific and a lot of time had to be spent on basics, like fitness. Now we are all professionals, and that shows in the fitness levels. Also everybody is much more aware of things like diet, and, sadly, the drinking is definitely a thing of the past. This time, everything is totally different – we've been together for the past six weeks.'

The atmosphere in the current camp impressed Alfie the most. 'In 1995 we were fairly downbeat. We lacked confidence. Nobody in the team expected us to compete with the likes of New Zealand. This year it's different, there's a great deal of self-belief in this squad.' The recent results, which had fostered this self-confidence, had also created an air of expectancy amongst the Welsh support. Were the players conscious of this? 'Yes, it is extra pressure, but then that's what we're paid for.' I also asked whether the squad were getting weary of the ceaseless round of training camps. 'Yeah,' he replied, 'we are all champing at the bit to get going. I know Graham wants us hungry for a game, and that is certainly the case at the moment. The preparations this time have been excellent, but we want to get out and perform. We can't wait for Argentina.'

The work in Portugal was certainly tough and the players were intensely focused on the job in hand. It would have been understandable if some of them were tiring from the constant training. Blackie played a key role here and was on his usual fine form, walking around with a permanent twinkle in his eye and always giving the impression that he was about to ease the mood in the camp with some prank. On one occasion, he emerged from the bushes and sneaked up behind Graham. 'And here we see the coach in his natural environment,' he whispered, in a breathless impersonation of David Attenborough. 'At first he may seem a little shy and defensive, but as we gain his confidence …' The narrative ran on for five minutes, a perfect parody of the 'Attenborough meets the gorilla family' episode. On another occasion, he had the entire squad in fits as he mercilessly destroyed an attempt at an interview by Eleri Sion of S4C's *Y Clwb Rygbi*.

The closeness of the squad was further illustrated on our last night in Portugal. After dinner at a local restaurant, Scott Gibbs led the players through a revivalist-type meeting, wherein they all attested to their conversion under their new leader. One after another the born-again players, urged on by the evangelical Mr Gibbs, testified to their reformation. The presentation was seamless, and had obviously been developed during the long period they had spent together. The normally quiet and retiring (off the field) Scott Gibbs was superb and obviously has a great future ahead of him, should Billy Graham ever require any assistance!

The players are an affable bunch, and they give readily of their time, whether it be to fans looking for autographs or journalists seeking interviews. However, one thing they are all aware of is just how susceptible they are to criticism, even when things are going well. I found this out first-hand after I filed some copy from Portugal, for *Wales on Sunday*. The paper had asked me to write some pieces, giving a view from inside the camp. A group of Welsh journalists came out to the camp on the Monday, and brought a copy of the paper with them.

The piece I had written was very positive, saying how hard the guys were working, and playing down the notion that this was some kind of holiday camp. The article was illustrated by shots of a penalty shoot-out competition that the boys had taken part in after training. Some of the players had a bit of a go at me over this. They maintained that some people would look at the pictures and, ignoring the text, would criticise the players for apparently spending their time messing about on a football field, when they should have been preparing for the World Cup. I thought they were being a bit oversensitive as the text made it clear that this was no holiday, but I could see their point. They had been caught before and were keen to avoid any situation which might be turned against them at a later date – a sad reflection of the relationship that has grown up between leading sportsmen and the media.

At the end of our stay in Portugal, Graham was satisfied with what had been achieved and felt that the trip had been worthwhile: 'I'd give it ten out of ten. The boys have been superb. They've really knuckled down and worked hard. The trip has allowed us to fine-tune a lot of areas of our game, and I think that we are better organised now than at any other time since I got here. It's given us the opportunity to work on areas such as the lineout, and to develop a few new plays. I think that we are as ready now as we could reasonably expect to be. There are a lot of variables that we cannot control, and much of what happens during the World Cup will be dictated by those elements. The boys are under a lot of pressure to perform. We don't know how they will react to the occasion.'

'In retrospect, what are your feelings about our warm-up games?' I asked him. 'Well, we didn't play very well, but at least we won. That's about all you can say. It's a tough one to call. We needed match practice, and the game against the French was really hard. Canada were also good opponents. It is all a question of balance. We have played a lot of Test matches in the last year, more than any other side. In some ways we could have done with a break, but then again we wouldn't want to be coming into the tournament not having played for three months. We've got a tough group; any one of three teams could win, so we have to stay focused now and just take each game as it comes. It's no good thinking ahead: the players must focus on one game at a time. We are much more disciplined now than we were at the beginning of last year's Five Nations. We had policies in place then, but I hadn't hammered them home enough. Today the boys are fully familiar with those policies and they should stick to them, even under pressure.'

The Dragon Awakes

We returned to Wales with ten days to go before the start of the tournament. One more week of training and the real business could begin. The players returned from Portugal refreshed, fit and raring to go. The months of preparation were finally over and the prospect of an opening game against Argentina didn't appear too daunting. The Welsh team had beaten Argentina, home and away, three times in the past season, and they had no reason to fear them now. The mood in the camp was quietly confident – but not over-confident.

SIX

THE RUGBY WORLD CUP

IT IS HARD TO BELIEVE NOW, but twelve years ago when the first Rugby World Cup was held in New Zealand and Australia, it was welcomed somewhat begrudgingly by many in the rugby fraternity. The Southern Hemisphere unions were the driving forces behind the competition, while the European unions dragged their feet and claimed there was no demand for such a tournament. Perhaps those in power in the North could see how the competition might drive the game forward and threaten their cosy world.

The first Rugby World Cup inspired very little interest outside the closed world of rugby, but it was the beginning of an event which, in twelve years, has become the third biggest sporting event in the world (after the football World Cup and the Olympics). In 1987 David Kirk lifted the Webb Ellis Trophy for New Zealand, who completely dominated the tournament. Once it got underway the inaugural tournament created great interest, and those who had predicted that it would be a one-off event were proved wrong. In 1987 Wales came third, defeating France courtesy of a late Paul Thorburn penalty. That remains Wales's best placement in the World Cup.

The Dragon Awakes

Four years later the tournament came to Britain. Here, the build-up was altogether more professional and the event attracted huge interest. I remember going to Twickenham for the opening match, between the holders, New Zealand, and the host nation, England. HQ was packed and I was offered four hundred pounds for my ticket, an indication of the interest created. For most people in Wales the 1991 tournament is remembered for the ignominious defeat of the national team at the hands of the Western Samoans.

The final was contested between England and Australia. It was another occasion where England let things slip. They had been impressive throughout the tournament, playing a forward-orientated game. Despite winning matches England attracted much criticism for their style of play. England responded to the criticism by changing their style and trying to play a more expansive game against Nick Farr-Jones's talented Australian team. This played right into the Aussies' hands, and they duly won the trophy. In the modern days of professionalism I cannot see any national coach making such a suicidal change.

The first two World Cups took place minus one of rugby's super-powers. By 1995 South Africa were back in the fold, and they hosted the third tournament. The World Cup in South Africa was dominated by New Zealand and saw the emergence of one of the games' great icons – Jonah Lomu. Lomu blew England away in the semi-final in an awesome display of power rugby. After that match no one could see anybody other than the All Blacks lifting the trophy but in the final the Kiwis were surprisingly lacklustre, and lost to the hosts. It was reported afterwards that a number of New Zealand players were suffering from a mysterious stomach bug. Whatever the reason for the New Zealanders' poor performance, the result was a PR man's dream. François Pienaar received the cup from Nelson Mandela, and the newly rejuvenated Rainbow Nation united behind its team.

THE SCENE IS SET. A COMPLETED MILLENIUM STADIUM AWAITS
THE OPENING MATCH OF THE 1999 RUGBY WORLD CUP.

THE WELSH TEAM LINE UP TO FACE SAMOA IN THE RUGBY WORLD CUP.
SAMOA CONTINUED THEIR JINX OVER WALES, WINNING THE MATCH
31–38.

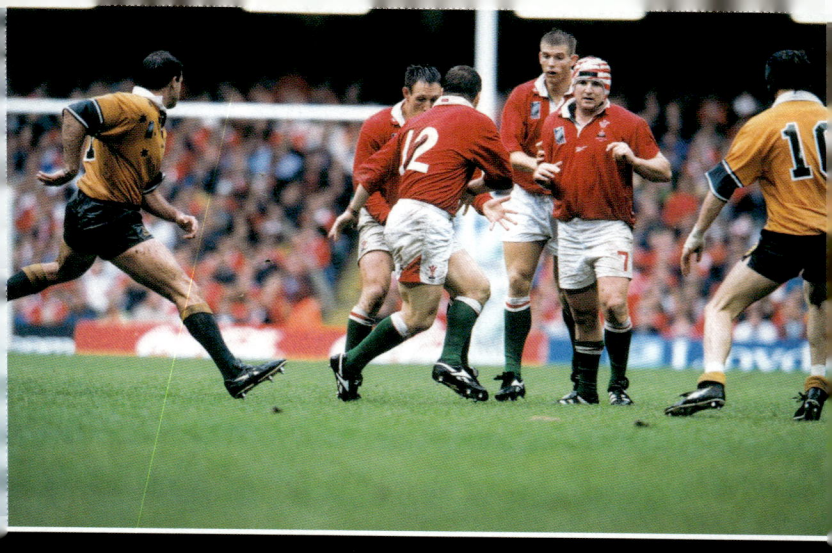

SCOTT GIBBS AND MARK TAYLOR SEARCH FOR A WAY TO UNLOCK THE AUSTRALIAN DEFENCE. BRETT SINKINSON AND DAFYDD JAMES LOOK ON.

ALLAN BATEMAN GETS THE BALL AWAY, DESPITE THE ATTENTIONS OF AUSTRALIA'S MATT BURKE

ABOVE AND BELOW: NEIL JENKINS, THE KICKING MACHINE, WHOSE ALL-ROUND GAME FLOURISHED UNDER THE LEADERSHIP OF GRAHAM HENRY.

ROB HOWLEY INSTIGATES ANOTHER ATTACK IN THE ROUT OF JAPAN IN THE RUGBY WORLD CUP.

CRAIG QUINELL GOES TO GROUND AGAINST JAPAN, WITH MARTYN WILLIAMS AND MIKE VOYLE IN CLOSE SUPPORT.

ABOVE: THE BRAINS BEHIND THE WELSH TEAM. GRAHAM HENRY AND STEVE BLACK IN THOUGHTFUL MOOD IN PORTUGAL.

LEFT: THE REDEEMER. GRAHAM HENRY OVERSEES A SESSION AT THE INDOOR TRAINING FACILITY AT PENCOED.

GRAHAM HENRY SHARES A JOKE WITH CHRIS WYATT AND CRAIG QUINELL.

A MOMENT OF RELAXATION BEFORE THE WORLD CUP. GRAHAM AND I ON THE TERRACE OF THE TEAM'S HEADQUARTERS IN PORTUGAL

FITNESS GURU STEVE BLACK. ONE OF THE DRIVING FORCES BEHIND THE WELSH RENAISSANCE.

PREPARING IN PORTUGAL. BEN EVANS LOOKS THOUGHTFUL, POSSIBLY TRYING TO UNDERSTAND COLIN CHARVIS'S DISTINCTIVE WELSH ACCENT.

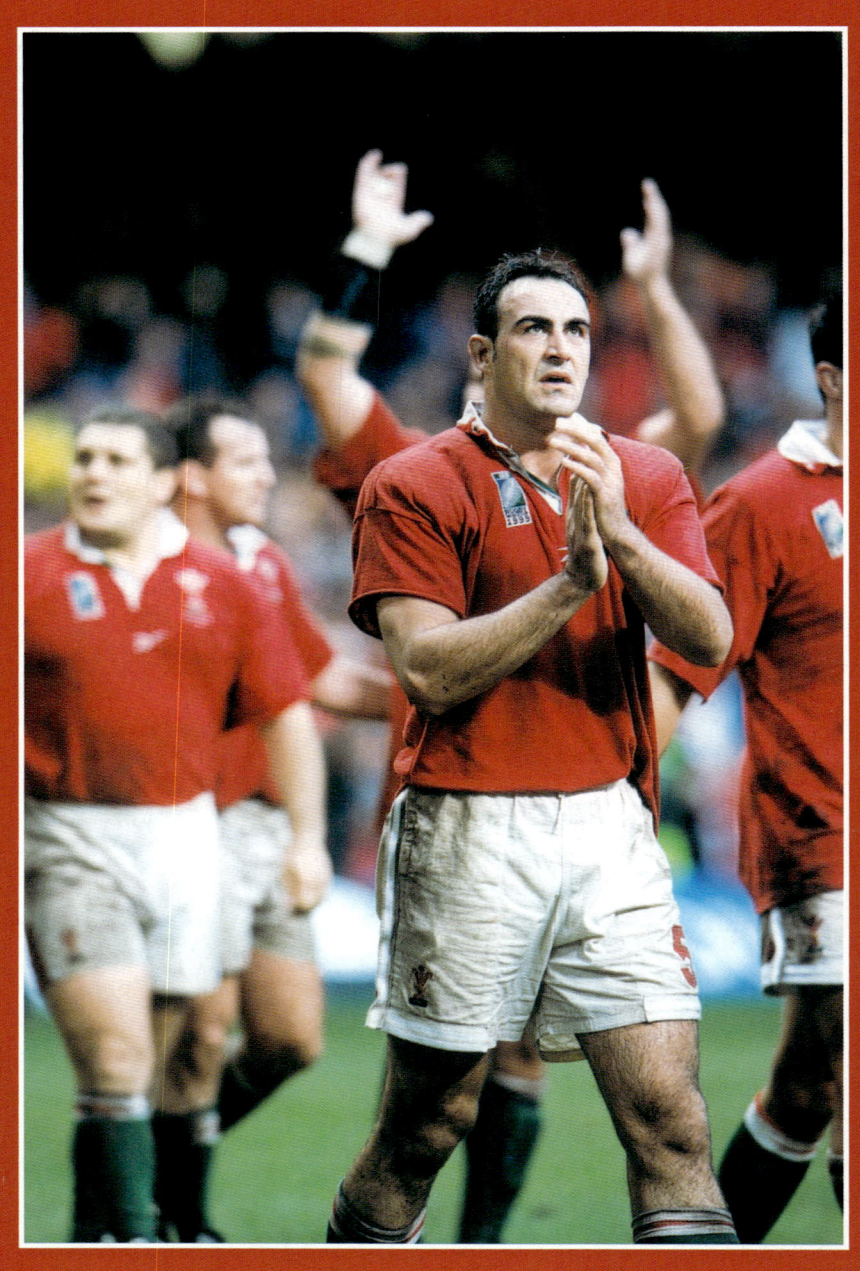

THE DREAM IS OVER! CHRIS WYATT'S FACE REVEALS THE DISAPPOINT-
MENT OF DEFEAT AGAINST AUSTRALIA, AND THE END OF WALES'S WORLD

The Dragon Awakes

The 1995 Rugby World Cup was significant in a number of ways. Firstly, it established the event as one of the world's major sporting competitions. It also saw the return of South Africa to the rugby fraternity.

Perhaps the most important result of the tournament was that it served as a watershed, bringing professionalism to the sport. It emerged that the Southern Hemisphere unions were in negotiations to set up trust funds for players. This meant that, in all but name, the leading players in South Africa, New Zealand and Australia were soon to be professionals. At the same time it was revealed that sixty of Europe's leading players had signed contracts committing them to taking part in an unauthorised professional rugby circus. The hands of the International Rugby Board were being forced, and the game rushed, somewhat precipitously, into professionalism.

From a Welsh perspective, the 1995 Rugby World Cup was another disappointment. Yet again we failed to make the knockout stages of the competition. Our only victory in South Africa came against Japan, and was followed by defeats against New Zealand and Ireland. This failure, following on from our defeat in 1991, prompted critics to the conclusion that Wales could no longer claim to be amongst the leading rugby nations. The decline of the Welsh team had become such that we were now a second division rugby team, who could only expect to win against the likes of Japan and Italy. This decline continued over the ensuing years, culminating in that nightmare game in Pretoria in 1998. Graham Henry had changed all that, and Wales were going into the fourth World Cup with heads held high, confident that they would at least make the quarter-final. As the hype around the team grew, there were many who felt that, with a bit of luck, Wales might just become the first Northern Hemisphere side to raise the Webb Ellis Trophy.

The buzz in the camp was tremendous in the final week of the build-up. As the opening match drew nearer, the tension amongst the players increased. The months of training, the practice matches and the video analysis had all been aimed towards that one date in October, when Wales would finally raise the curtain on the Rugby World Cup. The sense of anticipation was huge, and after months of preparation the players were itching to get under way. There was definitely a feeling that the players just wanted to get out and start playing. The World Cup was all they had thought about for the last three months, and there was almost a sense of relief that now, at last, they could get into action. There was tremendous media pressure building in Wales, and a great sense of expectancy throughout the country. The time for talking had come to an end, now it was time to deliver.

I feel that the attitude amongst most fans at the time was realistic: this Welsh team had improved beyond recognition in the previous year, but they had probably not improved enough to threaten the dominance of the Southern Hemisphere nations. Graham himself told me that his favourites for the competition were Australia and New Zealand.

Wales were expected to win their group, setting up a difficult quarter-final against Australia. However, as Graham had pointed out, we couldn't afford to be complacent. Our first game was against Argentina. We had beaten them three times in the past year, but they were capable of an upset on the day. Japan, even with a contingent of All Blacks in their ranks, shouldn't pose too much of a problem. Then there was Samoa, a nation that had become something of a bogey team to Wales in recent times.

Realistically, we should progress through the group stages and face the test of Australia in the quarter-finals. The optimists amongst us felt that if we could overcome Australia, we would probably face South Africa or England in the semi-final. We had beaten both of these teams in the last twelve months so victory was a possibility, leading to a final against New Zealand. The pessimists in the country envisaged us losing to Argentina and

THE DRAGON AWAKES

Samoa. I must admit that I took the middle road, feeling that we should win our group but that we would only defeat Australia if we were right on the edge and they were slightly off-peak.

While supporters across the country discussed the possible opponents we might come up against in the later stages, Graham's job was to keep the players focused on the Argentina game. He stressed that we must take one game at a time. If the players let their attention slip and started wondering about Australia in the quarter-finals or South Africa in the semis, we might well come unstuck.

In the build-up, Australia and New Zealand were evidently the teams to beat. In Rod Macqueen, Australia have one of the best-organised coaches in world rugby. This is reflected in their style of play. Their defence is superbly organised and they are excellent at shutting down opponents. Graham had come up against Macqueen when he was coaching the Auckland Blues and Macqueen was coach of ACT Brumbies, and he had the greatest respect for him. Australian rugby is on a high these days. The Australians have more than their fair share of world-class players. The midfield is particularly strong and they have three great game-breakers in Tim Horan, George Gregan and Stephen Larkham. Australia were captained by second-rower John Eales. An inspirational figure, Eales's importance to his team is indicated by his nickname – Nobody, as in 'Nobody's perfect'.

New Zealand had been going through something of a rebuilding process since the retirement of Sean Fitzpatrick. Earlier in the year they had suffered their worst losing run for fifty years. Coach John Hart responded by changing his back three. He moved Christian Cullen from full-back to wing, Jeff Wilson from wing to full-back, and brought in Tana Umaga on the other wing. Jonah Lomu, the most feared winger in world rugby, was moved to the bench. Lomu had recovered from his bout of terrible illness, and was back to his best. He is still the player that everyone wants to see, and he was bound to make an impact on the tournament yet again. Any combination of these four was certain to test out the best of defences.

South Africa were weaker than they had been in '95, but the Springboks would undoubtedly be desperate to hang on to the title of world champions. They had also recently enjoyed the longest winning run in world rugby, and their subsequent results may have had more to do with the psychological impact of that fact, than with any weaknesses in their playing strength. They would not give the title up easily, and it would be a foolish team that underestimated their ability.

Of the Northern Hemisphere teams, England and France represented the greatest threat to antipodean supremacy. However, France had had a disappointing Five Nations in 1999, and had not looked impressive in their build-up games. They seemed unsure as to what style of game they were trying to play. Even so, France had a set of backs capable of testing even the best of defences. If they got off to a good start, and the feeling in the camp was positive, their confidence would grow and they could pose a threat to the Southern Hemisphere dominance of the competition.

In Thomas Castaignède, France had one of the players who might yet become the player of the tournament. However, there is always a huge question mark over their mental attitude. When things are going well, the French can be awesome, but when their backs are against the wall they often go to pieces. I doubted whether they could put together the run of performances needed to lift the cup.

England were probably the dark horses of the tournament. Given their playing base, they should be able to put out a side capable of world domination, but this has not been achieved. Too often they appear to be on the brink of greatness only to disappoint. They certainly had the power and footballing ability to dominate any side up front. In Dallaglio, Back and Hill they have one of the finest back rows. They had experience in the shape of Jason Leonard and Martin Johnson, but there was a worry that their build-up had been too easy. They had played warm-up games against the USA and Italy, and had looked good in running up cricket scores. These matches had all the intensity of a training run, and I wondered whether they would have the hard edge to take on the best of the Southern Hemisphere sides.

Graham felt that Wales might have done the English a favour by beating them at Wembley. They lost that game in part as a result of complacency, and that should not be a danger for them again. He was certain that they would have learnt from the experience and would be a stronger team for it.

Scotland had won the Five Nations tournament in 1999, thanks to Wales's defeat of England, and had played some impressive rugby in doing so. If they could reproduce that form in the World Cup, they would be formidable opponents on their home patch at Murrayfield. Ireland appeared to be there just to make up the numbers, but you can never tell what the Irish will do. As for Wales, while my heart willed them to win, my money was firmly on New Zealand to take the trophy.

As October the First approached Graham Henry was not interested in talking about the chances of any of the competitors. He was adamant that the players must remain focused and take the tournament one game at a time. At the time his only concern was Argentina at the Millennium Stadium. The build-up to the opening match involved the normal training regime, but with fewer physical contact sessions. The squad trained on the Monday, Wednesday and Thursday prior to the match. The sessions were held at the Welsh Institute of Sport, at Sophia Gardens, Cardiff. The final sessions were held behind closed doors. The Welsh teams had developed a few new moves in Portugal, and Graham was keen to keep these under wraps, away from the prying eyes, and cameras, of the media. The tension in the team was building and there was less obvious jollity amongst the players. Even autograph signing was kept to a minimum.

The atmosphere in the camp had, I felt, less to do with apprehension concerning the opposition and more to do with the enormity of the occasion. We had beaten Argentina home and away over the last year, and the two teams knew each other well. Because of this familiarity Graham had little research to do, and his video analysis was not really too heavy a task. The Argentinian game revolves around their powerful pack. Graham Henry felt that Wales could compete in this area, but also that Wales had more variety and versatility at their disposal. The game plan involved playing the game on opposition territory, and then playing at pace to unsettle the strong, but slow, Argentinian forwards. The recent history suggested that Wales would simply have too much firepower for the one-dimensional Argentinians.

The day was more about the overall occasion than simply about a rugby match. This would be the first game played at a full Millennium Stadium. Given the atmosphere in the ground when it was only half-full, the opening game promised to be a passionate and noisy affair. The weather was kind to the organisers, and Cardiff was buzzing several hours before the kick-off. Thousands of ticketless supporters rolled into town to watch the game on the large screens situated at a number of venues around the city. Rock and jazz bands played on the street corners, as testimony to Wales's newly established reputation as a force in the popular music industry.

By 1.30 p.m., there was a large crowd gathered in the stadium for the opening ceremony. This was an unashamedly Welsh affair. In addition to the usual male voice choirs, there were performances from two of Wales's perennial favourites, Shirley Bassey and Max Boyce. The largest roar was saved for a parade of ex-international players. Cerys Matthews with Catatonia fired up the crowd with a glittering rendition of their song 'International Velvet'. Today, of all days, the song's refrain of

The Dragon Awakes

'Everyday when I wake up I thank the Lord I'm Welsh', seemed particularly apposite. After the pyrotechnics of the opening ceremony, the pitch was cleared and the stage was set for the opening of the tournament.

Unfortunately, as a spectacle the match failed to live up to its build-up, something which could easily have been predicted. The players appeared apprehensive and jittery. Even Neil Jenkins appeared to be affected by nerves, as he missed his opening penalty opportunity. After twenty-five minutes Argentina were leading 6–0, and the Welsh team were looking decidedly out of sorts. Then Jenkins brought the scores level with two penalties, and Wales started to play with a little more control. The Argentinian outside half, Gonzalo Quesada, put the visitors ahead again, but in the first minute of injury time Colin Charvis barged over under the posts, bringing the crowd to life. Jenkins converted and Wales went into half-time leading 13–9.

At half-time, Graham emphasised the need to take control of the game. The Argentinians were dictating the pace of the game too much: they were kicking at every opportunity, meaning that we were not getting the field position that we wanted. The plan was to play at pace and take them on with ball in hand.

In the second half the boys settled down a little and played some good rugby. For a period of about a quarter of an hour, Wales played intense, flowing rugby and completely dominated the visitors. Mark Taylor scored an excellent try and Wales looked like they might sweep the opposition away, but then three or four chances went begging and Wales went off the boil. A Jenkins penalty took the Welsh to twenty-three points, and a fourteen-point lead. Then, as the home side relaxed, Quesada kicked Argentina back into contention with three more penalties. Wales rallied towards the end, and held out to record their ninth successive victory, with a final score of 23–18, and get the World Cup campaign off to a victorious start.

Graham was not particularly pleased by the result and refused

THE DRAGON AWAKES

to accept any excuses for the lacklustre performance. 'Sure, we were rusty,' he told me on the following Monday. 'The conditions were not ideal for playing running rugby, and the occasion may have got to them. But we should have done better. This is a new position for the players. They're part of a successful team, and many opposition teams will take a negative approach towards them. They have to adapt to this. Most worrying is the fact that we should be putting teams like Argentina away. We were on top, but we lacked the killer instinct. Teams like South Africa, Australia and the All Blacks finish teams off when they are in the ascendancy. We are not used to doing this. It's a problem we have to address.'

Apart from the media's analysis of Wales's performance against Argentina, the major point of discussion was the citing of Colin Charvis for throwing a punch during the match. Charvis had retaliated when attacked by a member of the Argentine front row. At the time the referee, Paddy O'Brien, had threatened the visiting prop, Roberto Grau, with a yellow card but had said nothing to Charvis. After the game Charvis was cited by an IRB official who had been sitting in the stand. This was to be policy throughout the World Cup: a fourth official at each match could cite players for foul or dangerous play.

Many people in the media welcomed the move as a way of keeping acts of violence out of the game. Others were less convinced. Graham Henry was amongst the latter group. 'OK, it might be a good idea in principle but it has to be consistent. If Charvis deserved to be cited, then so did several others. The referee saw the incident, and he didn't even talk to Charv about it. It's a ridiculous situation. The IRB are making a rod for their own backs with this one, and I doubt they will be able to make it work.'

It appears to me that citing may be valid with reference to off-the-ball incidents, things that may be missed by referees and linesmen because they take place away from the action. Charvis's misdemeanour occurred right under the referee's nose, and he chose not to punish the players involved. If a spectator is to be allowed to overrule the referee's decision, his authority will be undermined. I think the same is true of the use of video replays to back up a referee's decision. Too often the video replay is inconclusive, and the very presence of some kind of higher authority undermines the position of the man on the field. Referees are not perfect, and they will make mistakes, but for the most part they get it right and it's as good a system as we can hope for.

Like it or not, the citing system was here for the duration of the World Cup, and Colin Charvis was its first victim: he got a two-match ban. Graham publicly supported Charvis and reiterated his doubts about the entire citing procedure. The players also made their feelings about the incident clear. After scoring against Japan, Gareth Thomas took off his rugby shirt to reveal a 'Free Colin Charvis' T-shirt. But behind the scenes, I am fairly certain that Charvis got something of a roasting from the team coach. Graham had always stressed the need for discipline and control on the field. Charvis had broken that ordinance, and I was sure that he had been duly rebuked. When I raised the question with Graham he would say nothing, but the look on Dai Pickering's face told me that I was probably correct in my notion that facing the disciplinary board had been a doddle for Charv compared to the meeting he had with Graham.

The Charvis incident was a sideshow, and Graham could not afford to be distracted from the main event. Eight days after playing Argentina, Wales had to face Japan. Normally one would expect us to beat Japan pretty easily, but Graham was warning against complacency. The Japanese have always been known for playing attractive running, but losing, rugby. They simply lack the physical presence needed to compete at the top level. This time, though, the Japanese side was given a bit more steel by the inclusion of four New Zealanders in the side, including the two ex-All Blacks, Jamie Joseph and Graeme Bachop. In addition, they had done very well in the World Cup qualifying rounds and had beaten Samoa recently. However, in their opening match of the tournament Japan had lost 43–9 to Samoa, and it looked as if they were to be the whipping boys of the group.

Graham Henry was cautious not because he thought Wales might lose, but because they might not win by enough. Wales were in a tough group, and progression to the next round might depend on how many points each team scored against Japan. He had already voiced his concerns about Wales's lack of ruthlessness against lesser teams, and our situation going into the Japan game was a fine illustration of the need for Wales to develop a harder edge. Our poor performance against Argentina, and the need to score points against Japan, stopped Graham from making wholesale changes to the team. The Japanese match would be a good chance to give second-string players a run out, but on the other hand Wales could not afford to disrupt the pattern of play.

Graham told me he would make only six changes for the match. He had to find a replacement for Charvis, at blind side flanker, so Martyn Williams was in. Jason Jones-Hughes would get his first start in a Welsh jersey, and Allan Bateman was to play on the wing. Chris Wyatt was to be rested and replaced by Mike Voyle, with Geraint Lewis coming in to replace Scott Quinnell. Graham was treading a fine line, torn between the need for stability and the desire to keep all the boys involved, and fuelled by the desire to look for new combinations and ideas.

The team finally selected to play Japan had stability in the front row and in midfield. On a number of occasions, Graham emphasised to me the need to develop a strong and stable backbone within a team. This backbone starts with the front three, goes back through the number 8 and the half-backs, to the centres and full-back. When it is well established, you should not tinker with the backbone of a team; changes outside this area tend to be less drastic in their effects. From this point of view, the only major change was the inclusion of Geraint Lewis, replacing Scott Quinnell. Lewis is a superb footballing number 8, and his playing style was well suited to the sort of game Wales would play against Japan.

The game plan against Japan was similar to that against Argentina. The idea was that Wales would take them on with the ball in hand. 'We should be able to dominate them up front, and then take the ball through quick phases of play,' Henry explained. 'It's not hugely different from what we tried to do against Argentina. The only difference is we have to do it better.' Graham had criticised his team after the Argentina match for not putting the opposition away, and for lacking the killer instinct which is necessary in a great team. He really pushed this point in the build-up to the Japan game. 'We must remember that in the event of a three-way tie in our group, it will be the side who scores most against Japan that will win the group, so we must finish well against the Japanese. We can't afford to get sloppy once the game is won. We need points.'

It would be possible, especially with the advantage of hindsight, to draw the conclusion that Graham lacked confidence in his team. Did he feel that Samoa were too strong for Wales? Possibly. I think it is more likely that this is just another manifestation of Graham's refusal to leave anything to chance. When I pushed him on the matter he simply said: 'I don't like to think that we will lose to Samoa, but I have to take the possibility into my calculations. I'd look pretty bloody stupid after the event if I didn't.'

The Welsh nation puts tremendous – some would say unreasonable – pressure on its rugby team. Rugby, for many, is what defines the Welsh nation. It is the area where, historically, we have been able to compete on an equal footing with the best, and with England. After the defeats against Scotland and Ireland, Graham began to comprehend the importance of rugby to the

The Dragon Awakes

Welsh nation and the concomitant pressure this placed on the national team. 'I couldn't believe it,' he said after the Scottish defeat. 'Guys went home and didn't open their front door for two or three days. All because of the pressure they felt at having let the supporters down. Jesus, who needs that.'

Since then, the pressure on the Welsh team had increased. Fifteen months before the World Cup they had been no-hopers. Many people felt that the biggest challenge facing Welsh rugby was getting the stadium built in time for the tournament – having a team worthy of playing in that stadium simply wasn't on the agenda. Graham Henry had changed all that. He had given the Welsh squad a sense of self-belief, which had then passed on to the nation. Suddenly, people were not just talking about Wales doing well; they were talking of winning the tournament. Whereas nine months ago any victory was grasped with eager hands, now the supporters were beginning to demand that Wales win with style and élan. The fans wanted to see the panache that we had demonstrated in the first half in Paris, or the passionate commitment we had shown against South Africa.

The pressure, along with other factors on the day, had taken its toll on the players in the opening game. The eyes of the world were on Cardiff, and the occasion may have been too much for some. Blackie had also been taken ill during the game. Given the strength of the bond between the players and their fitness coach, this may have affected their performance. Against Japan, this pressure was lifted slightly, or, at least, it was lifted for fourteen of the guys taking the field. In the build-up to the Japanese game the talk was not about whether or not we could win, or whether we could put fifty points on the Japanese – the big question was whether Jenks could overtake Michael Lynagh to become the highest points scorer in world rugby. Lynagh held the record, with 911 points. Jenkins was in second place with 892. He needed twenty points against Japan in order to take the record, and given that it was anticipated that Wales would score quite a few tries, there would be plenty of conversions to give Jenks a chance. With all eyes on Jenkins, the other players were able to enter the match feeling more relaxed. This showed in the game, which was uneven but generally satisfactory.

However, Graham's worry about Wales's failure to put teams away raised its head again in the Japan game. The problem stems from the fact that Wales continue to play their rugby in bursts. For the first half-hour they played excellently against Japan, and built up a commanding lead. Then they seemed to go to sleep. Unforced errors were seized upon by the Japanese and they clawed their way back into the match through tries by Ohata and Tuidraki. Stern words from Mr Henry during the half-time interval served to wake the team up for the second half, and the guys came out and played some vintage rugby. Shane Howarth was the instigator of much of the play in the second half, as Wales attacked, ball in hand, from even the deepest positions.

The day had gone well for Wales. The final score of 64–15 would surely have given them the cushion they needed to win the group, whatever happened against Samoa. The manner of the win was satisfactory, and Henry had used all his substitutes during the game, thereby keeping the whole squad involved. Wales had scored nine tries. Jenkins had converted eight of these, and slotted a penalty, for a personal tally of 19 points. This brought his career total to 911 points, level with Michael Lynagh's record. He had got tantalisingly close to becoming the world's leading points scorer, but now he would have to wait until the Samoan game to break the record.

The tournament was now well and truly underway. There had been sixteen matches played, no major upsets and the leading teams were beginning to find their form. The game of the tournament so far had unquestionably been England v New

THE DRAGON AWAKES

Zealand. England had pushed the All Blacks, at a packed Twickenham, but they lacked the steel to finish the New Zealanders off and that man Lomu had done it again.

In Wales, the tournament was a huge success. It dominated daily life in the Principality. There was wall-to-wall coverage on television and in the newspapers, and it was the only topic of conversation in pubs up and down the country. However, looking at the matches being played in the other host nations it was apparent that these countries had not taken the event to heart in quite the same way. Televised matches showed a half-empty Murrayfield. The World Cup seemed to be causing little in the way of a buzz at Twickenham, apart from the All Blacks game, and a similar indifference was apparent in Ireland and France.

There had been much worry prior to the event about Wales's ability to host the tournament. What now became apparent was that the entire tournament should have been held here. Wales's matches at the new Millennium Stadium were automatic sell-outs, but the games not involving the hosts were also very well attended. Argentina, Japan and Samoa played matches at Wrexham and at Stradey Park, Llanelli, and at both venues the Welsh turned out in huge numbers to size up the opposition.

This triggered off a debate about the way tickets are allocated, a perennial gripe amongst Welsh supporters. The claim is that too many tickets are issued under the banner of corporate hospitality. This results in a crowd made up of businessmen on freebies, while the real fans are forced to watch the game on television. This argument just doesn't hold water. The reality is that many people who claim to be true rugby fans are, in truth, only interested in going to internationals. Evidence for this is supplied by the level of support at club games, where most teams enjoy crowds of only two or three thousand. Those people, and the players who turn up week in, week out for junior clubs, are the real, grass roots supporters of the game in Wales.

If you are a member of a club, either as a player or a spectator, you have a realistic chance of getting international tickets. I am a member of both Ebbw Vale RFC and Gwernyfed RFC, my local junior side. I coach at club and county level. I rarely have a problem getting hold of a ticket, and I would argue that I earn my allocation of tickets for major games. Those people who complain that they never get tickets should do their bit to support junior rugby on a regular basis. They might then find that, miraculously, tickets are not so hard to come by.

The ticketing arrangements for the matches in Cardiff were not ideal, and the WRU seemed to struggle to get tickets out on time. The confusion this caused was unforgivable, and must be addressed. The World Cup is one of the world's largest sporting occasions, and the WRU might have struggled to host the entire event, but splitting the World Cup between five nations made it too disparate and much of its impact was lost.

I would also question the timing of the matches. Wales played two of their three qualifying matches on a weekday. The World Cup was a golden opportunity to get the children of the nation involved in the national game, but it was organised in such a way that the home team played when children were in school, and the rest of the nation was supposed to be at work. Presumably, medical records will show that there were many mystery illnesses sweeping the country at this time, and that there has never been a higher demand for medical certificates!

Wales had now won ten matches back to back, an achievement that was unthinkable twelve months before, adding to the pressure the players were feeling going into the Samoan game. Samoa had beaten Wales in the 1991 World Cup, and this defeat had been responsible for the team failing to proceed to the knockout stages of the tournament. At the time, the defeat had been seen as a major upset. Many Welsh supporters in the early 1990s were still deludedly hanging on to the notion that we were a world force in the game, and that our rightful place was alongside New Zealand and Australia. Many made light of the defeat with the comment that it was just as well we were only playing Western Samoa, not the whole country. Samoa had won again at the next meeting of the two nations, and were now looking for a hat-trick of wins over Wales.

If we had taken them lightly in '91, there was no chance of that happening in '99. There was a collective desire to make up for the previous embarrassing defeats. Also, the present Samoan team contained a number of players for whom the Welsh management had tremendous respect. Pat Lam and Va'aiga Tuigamala had worked with Graham in New Zealand, and with Blackie at Newcastle Falcons. Graham and Blackie could not speak highly enough of the two Samoan veterans, and there was a strong feeling that these two old heads might come up with something to upset the host nation. 'Pat and Inga are both top guys,' Graham told me. 'Great players, and we would be foolish to take anything for granted against them.'

Against Samoa, the game plan needed to be strictly adhered to. They like to play a fast and furious style of rugby, and have gained a deserved reputation for aggressive defence. Their players really relish the opportunity to put in big hits on their opponents, and by doing so they put other teams under pressure. They are less at home against opposition who take control of a game. They can be dominated in the tight, and the answer is to play percentage rugby against them. Keep the game tight, and keep mistakes down to a minimum.

As could have been predicted, Wales did this in part, but made too many mistakes. The forwards established dominance early on, and Wales gained field position, enabling them to put the Samoans under pressure. Jenkins missed an early penalty, which would have given him the world record. Finally, after thirteen minutes, Wales were awarded a penalty try, which Jenks converted to ease ahead of Lynagh in the points scoring stakes. Shortly afterwards, Gareth Thomas crossed in the corner and Wales seemed to be taking hold of the match.

The Dragon Awakes

Graham had warned that Samoa would punish any Welsh errors and this seemed prophetic when a poor throw-in from Garin Jenkins soared over Chris Wyatt's outstretched arms for Lio Falaniko to collect and fall over the Welsh try-line. Suddenly, Samoa were back in the game. They upped the pace and harried Wales at every opportunity. The Samoan defence stood very flat, perilously close to offside, and benefited by scoring two interception tries. Between these two tries, Stephen Bachop orchestrated another score from a backline move. In the last quarter Wales rallied and started to control the game, with Jenkins going for field position and the Welsh forwards performing well in the tight and the loose. Wales dominated at the scrummage and won another penalty try for their efforts. In the dying minutes Wales forced another scrum on the Samoan line but, yet again, their control let them down. The ball squirted out of the side of the scrum and the chance was lost. The Samoan bogey had struck again.

Graham's explanation of the defeat was brief and to the point: 'We made too many basic errors, and that put us under tremendous pressure.' In reality, Wales had lost the game rather than Samoa winning it. We had gifted the game to them through lack of control. The winning streak had been placing unnecessary pressure on the team, and Graham had hinted to me that Wales needed to lose a game in order to stop thinking about winning runs and focus on each individual match.

Somehow, Graham's words didn't ease the pain of defeat, either for players or spectators. However, at least it didn't mean the end of our World Cup as it had in '91. Wales were still certain to qualify for the knockout stages. Now, the question was whether they would go through as group winners or as the second-place team. Our final position in the group would be determined by the result of the Argentina–Japan game. If Argentina could score sixty-nine points against Japan, they would top the group. In that event Wales were faced with a difficult trip up to Murrayfield to play Scotland in the play-offs. This was to be avoided on two counts. Firstly, winning against Scotland on their home patch would be a difficult task, and secondly it meant an extra game, something all the players felt they most definitely didn't need.

Consequently, the following Saturday the Welsh nation got behind Japan as they faced up to the Pumas at the Millennium Stadium. Argentina are not famed for their flowing, attacking play, and it seemed unlikely that they could score the necessary points. In the event, Argentina could only manage thirty-three points against Japan's twelve, so Wales had won the group and would face Australia in the quarter-final.

Australia, New Zealand and South Africa had started the tournament as favourites. So far, Australia had cruised through the tournament without ever being stretched. Their defence was particularly strong, they had only conceded thirty-one points in reaching the quarter-finals, and they had a backline full of strong and elusive runners. To beat them, Wales would have to play at the top of their game. As Blackie pointed out, if both teams played to their full potential you would still have to fancy Australia, but on the day anything can happen.

The atmosphere for the match was the best of the tournament, even surpassing the opening ceremony. That had been an event: this was a real match! The roar from the crowd as Howley led his team out was truly deafening; the players said afterwards that it was impossible to hear calls for each play. The game gave a clear indication of what Graham Henry and his team had achieved in a little over twelve months. It also showed just how far they still needed to go.

If Wales were to upset the Australians they would need control and focus. The aim of the game had to be to gain possession and then hold on to it. Graham was looking for the team to develop into one that could string together nine, ten or eleven phases of play. Patience is the key: players must not become anxious and try to force the opening – keep the ball moving through repeated phases and wait for the gap to appear.

On the day, the Welsh team threw everything they had at the Australians. Wales played with vigour and commitment in a marvellously spirited match. But however hard they tried, the Australian defence refused to crack. After much early pressure from Wales, George Gregan sneaked in at the corner to give Australia an early lead. As the rain started to fall Jenkins opened the scoring for Wales with a penalty, which was answered by a kick from Matt Burke.

By the mid-point of the first half the rain was torrential, and it was becoming apparent that the Australians were not happy playing in good, old-fashioned Welsh weather. The Australian back three looked very uncomfortable under the high ball, and Wales enjoyed a period of sustained pressure. This begs a question about the much-vaunted skill of Southern Hemisphere teams. We are told that we cannot compete with them on basic ball-handling skills. Australia and South Africa in particular are used to playing in dry conditions, on hard pitches. What was apparent in Cardiff was that the Australians were not able to adjust easily to the wetter conditions more normally found in Europe. What couldn't be faulted on the day, though, was the awesome defensive organisation of the Aussies. They beat back wave after wave of attacks from the determined Welsh. Again, this brings the inventiveness of the Welsh attack into question. With the Australians unhappy with a ball which was rapidly becoming as slippery as a bar of wet soap, why didn't Wales try chip kicks and grubbers to turn the redoubtable Australian defence?

In that first half Wales scored through three penalties from Jenkins, and it has to be said that penalties seemed to be the only way we could score. The work rate amongst the Welsh forwards was immense, but this was really a case of the irresistible force meeting the immovable object, and the immovable Australian defence was winning the day. The second half continued in the same vein. Wales stuck patiently to their game, hoping that eventually gaps would appear. However, this time the Australians were even more disciplined in defence, and refused to give away kickable penalties. With our main scoring weapon immobilised, Wales had nothing to offer in terms of scoring. Australia, on the other hand, looked more incisive, and scored tries through Ben Tune and Gregan. This last should never have been allowed, as everybody in the stadium, apart from referee Colin Hawke, saw a massive knock-on by Australia. I also had my doubts about the validity of Gregan's first try, as the ball appeared to be deliberately taken back into the ruck. However, one could argue about the scoreline but not about the eventual result. On the day, Australia were the better side. The Welsh team were obviously disappointed, but they should feel proud of themselves for the performance, which was light years away from what they had been doing eighteen months earlier.

My equanimity about the result was not shared by most Welsh supporters, who felt that we had been robbed of victory by the New Zealand referee. It was sad to hear chants of 'cheat' echoing around the ground after his bad decision to award Gregan's second try. Hawke had a nightmarish game, but his was an honest mistake and, in all honesty, it didn't affect the result. Many Welsh supporters insisted after the match that the Australian defence had appeared good because they had lived offside. I found it hard to believe that a referee of Hawke's standing could have missed out on the Australians consistently standing offside. My belief was strengthened after a conversation with Clive Norling, the WRU's Director of Referees. Norling told me that he had studied videos of the game immediately after the match, and after repeated viewings he was forced to conclude that Hawke and his linesmen had done a good job – the Australian defence had indeed been onside for the majority of the match.

The Dragon Awakes

What the match highlighted was the importance of defence in modern rugby. Increasingly, the key to winning matches lies in having a well organised defence. The Australians and New Zealanders never commit too many players at breakdown situations. They only commit three or four players to each ruck: the other forwards move into midfield. Once the ball is lost, players lie off the ruck and line up in preparation for the next wave of attack. The Australians are superb in this respect. It is an area where we have learnt a great deal from rugby league. The return of players such as Allan Bateman and Scott Gibbs from the thirteen-man code has done much to improve standards at senior level, but I doubt that enough attention is paid to defence in junior rugby. Many leading Welsh teams are now employing defence coaches, but greater emphasis on defence at junior levels would improve the overall standard of play throughout the country.

At the end of the match, our dreams of World Cup success lay shattered. Realistically, few of us had felt that we could win the tournament, and there was no dishonour in the manner of our defeat. We had lost to a great Australian side and the players had given everything for the national cause. For ten minutes, the players stayed on the field and were given a standing ovation by the supporters. As the players saluted their fans, I could feel a lump rising in my throat, knowing how much effort and emotion the boys had put into the tournament. You could see that this defeat really hurt; the emotion was evident on the faces of the players. The reaction of the crowd was symptomatic of the change in Welsh rugby. The fans stood squarely behind the team, even in defeat. There was none of the customary sniping and carping. The fans realised that the team had done its best: it simply wasn't enough. Defeat by Australia was eased by the fact that they went on to win the tournament. The World Cup had not been an unqualified success, both from a Welsh perspective and in general terms. Spreading the tournament over a number

The Dragon Awakes

of countries had not been a good idea, and as a result the event became diluted. There was poor support in the venues outside Wales, especially Scotland, and matches not involving the home nations were sidelined. The games were badly arranged in terms of timing, with long periods of inactivity. Four- or five-day lapses, with no matches, prevented the tournament from picking up impetus. On the positive side there were a number of memorable matches, notably the semi-final between New Zealand and France, and a lot of great tries were scored.

The Welsh team were disappointed in going out at the quarter-final stage, but their honour had been restored. Wales could no longer be viewed as the whipping boys of world rugby. Our loss against the eventual winners could be viewed as an honourable defeat. Under Graham Henry's management team, Welsh rugby had undoubtedly improved. However, the overall pecking order within the game had changed little. Undoubtedly, the World Cup underlined the continued dominance of the Southern Hemisphere nations. The only European side to reach the semi-finals was France, and although they beat New Zealand in a pulsating game, no one doubts that currently the best three sides in world rugby are Australia, New Zealand and South Africa. As they proved in the semi-final, on the day France can beat anyone, but they are also capable of losing to anyone. England are certainly on a par with France, and not far behind South Africa. What is questionable about England is their ability to think on their feet. Poor decision-making cost them the game on that memorable day in Wembley. It also contributed to their defeat by South Africa in the quarter-final of the World Cup. England had the players to win that match, but they were unable to adapt their game plan to outwit the less talented but more astute South Africans.

For a rugby fanatic living in Wales, the event was tremendous. The atmosphere around Cardiff on match days was electric. The new Millennium Stadium was a tremendous success, and has

The Dragon Awakes

already become accepted as part of the great rugby tradition in Wales. All that is needed for complete acceptance by the fans is a different name; it will always be seen as the Arms Park. We saw some great rugby, and while we didn't win the tournament, we did lay the foundations for a side which should compete in 2003.

For the players the tournament was draining, both emotionally and physically. It had been their focus for the past twelve months and suddenly it was over. In an ideal world they should all have disappeared for some well-earned rest and recuperation. However, the world of professional rugby is far from ideal. These players are on large salaries, paid for by clubs who had done without the services of their stars for the opening months of the domestic season. Consequently, they were rushed back into action with irreverent haste. With a few exceptions the entire squad was press-ganged back into action playing domestic rugby. The repercussions of this would be felt in a very short time.

SEVEN

INTERMISSION

THROUGHOUT THE WORLD CUP the Welsh–Scottish Premier League had rolled on without the services of its leading players. Graham Henry had made much of the fact that the structure of domestic rugby was not conducive to building a strong national team. He believed that players were playing too many matches, too many of which were uncompetitive. This problem had been addressed to an extent by inviting the two Scottish super-districts to play in the Welsh Premiership. The league had been further strengthened with the return to the fold of Cardiff and Swansea after their abortive attempts to join the English Allied Dunbar Premiership. Cardiff and Swansea had not performed well in the opening months of the season, largely due to them missing the many stars who were off on World Cup duty. Pontypridd and Ebbw Vale took advantage of this situation and both sides were going well in the newly revamped league.

While the Welsh–Scottish League was a distinct improvement on the Welsh League of the previous year, it was still far from the finished article. The Scottish districts were not strong enough to challenge for honours, and Caerphilly and Dunvant were propping up the league. Neither side was really capable of competing at this level.

The gulf between the Welsh First Division and the Premiership has become too great. Dunvant had done well in winning the First Division the previous season, but to be expected to compete with the star-studded line-ups at clubs like Cardiff, Swansea and Llanelli is asking too much. The promoted team doesn't have time to build a competitive squad in the build-up to its first season at the top, and consequently immediate relegation is very likely. This was certainly the case during the 1999–2000 season. The relegation battle was obviously going to involve two teams, Caerphilly and Dunvant.

What became apparent after the return of the international players was that the Welsh league contained a nucleus of seven clubs capable of competing at the highest level. Newport had taken advantage of the resources of its millionaire backer to build a formidable multi-national side, led by Gary Teichmann. Cardiff and Swansea took some time to meld into a working unit after the World Cup, but Llanelli were as competitive as ever, and Pontypridd and Ebbw Vale continued to remind everybody that they underrated the unfashionable sides at their peril. Neath were building a competitive side, built around the attacking talents of a number of youngsters.

The European competitions looked to be dominated by the French, but Welsh sides were acquitting themselves honourably. Cardiff and Llanelli were unlucky to come up against one another at the quarter-final stage. Llanelli demolished Cardiff 22–3, before losing to the eventual winners, Northampton. In the Shield, Ebbw Vale flew the flag for Wales: after winning all their games in the group stage of the competition, they were unlucky to lose by a point, in injury time, to London Irish. These games served their purpose in highlighting the talents of a number of players who hadn't featured in Graham Henry's plans earlier in the year. I spoke to Graham at the Ebbw Vale v Toulon game, and he was impressed by the Ebbw half-backs and Nathan Budgett. The half-backs, Richard Smith and Jason Strange, eventually made it into the squad for the Six Nations, and Budgett finished the season as a member of the Welsh team. Others staking a claim included Neath's Shane Williams, Alix Popham of Newport, Cardiff's Rhys Williams and Matt Cardey of Llanelli.

The domestic game was strengthened during the 1999–2000 season, but as preparation for international rugby it was a disaster. The Welsh internationals who had given their all for the country during the World Cup returned home and were expected to pull out all the stops in order to ensure their clubs a coveted place in Europe. By the time the international season came around in February 2000, the country's leading players had been playing non-stop rugby for fifteen months. During that time they had played seventeen internationals, numerous club matches in the domestic league and European competitions, as well as taking part in a rigorous training regime in preparation for the World Cup. It was a battle-weary squad that gathered in early February in preparation for the Six Nations tournament.

EIGHT

THE SIX NATIONS

WHATEVER THE PLAYERS MAY HAVE FELT, Welsh rugby fans awaited the start of the Six Nations tournament with excited anticipation. The Rugby World Cup had, if possible, increased the appetite for the game in Wales, and there was a strong belief that we could do very well in the first international event of the new millennium. The season saw the inclusion of Italy in the tournament for the first time. Italy had been lobbying for inclusion for many years. Recently they had defeated Ireland and Scotland, and they gave Wales a scare in 1998, losing narrowly, 23–20, at Stradey Park. Unfortunately for them, before and during the World Cup it became apparent that they were not as strong currently as they had been in past seasons, and no one saw them as much of a threat to the more established nations. Scotland and Ireland had not impressed in the World Cup, which meant that France and England were firm favourites to lift the title. England had not done as well as they would have liked in the World Cup, but they were still viewed by many as the strongest team in the Northern Hemisphere. France should have been riding high after making the final in November, but their coach, Jean-Claude Skrela, had resigned following their defeat by Australia and the new coach, Bernard Laporte, was an unknown quantity at international level. Wales had defeated France on their last two meetings and had beaten England the previous season. This gave cause for optimism amongst the rugby-watching public in Wales. Maybe this year we would be able to challenge for the championship.

Graham organised a trial match at Swansea, a week prior to the opening game against France. About a hundred players took part, but there were few revelations. Graham had talked a lot about the lack of strength in depth in Welsh rugby. The players on trial showed that this problem had lessened during the past twelve months, but it was evident that the usual suspects were likely to be selected against France. Shane Williams and Nathan Budgett reproduced their club form and showed themselves as potential internationals, but the team that Graham announced for the French Test was pretty predictable. Injuries to Scott Gibbs and Craig Quinnell forced two changes; Jason Jones-Hughes came in for Gibbs, with Ian Gough replacing Quinnell. The significant change was in the captaincy. Rob Howley's captaincy had been one of the lines of continuity maintained by Graham Henry when he took charge of Wales in 1998. Now Howley was relieved of the captaincy, and replaced by David Young. Although the change was reported in the media as a shock decision, it was not really that surprising. Howley had been a tremendously successful captain, leading Wales to fifteen victories, including a winning run of ten games, but his own form had suffered during the World Cup. Howley is potentially one of the best scrum-halves in world rugby, but he appeared to have lost his edge in recent internationals. The spark that had made him such a dangerous opponent seemed to have been dimmed by the responsibilities of captaincy.

According to Henry, 'At his best, Rob Howley is a fantastic footballer. He's a game-breaker. I felt the captaincy was affecting his play. He doesn't express himself so well on the field when he is also having to think about other people's games.' This was underlined by his performances for Cardiff. At club level, where he was not captain, Howley was in dynamic form, and this prompted Graham to make the change.

The timing of the decision was queried by a number of pundits, who claimed that Henry could have made the announcement earlier rather than dropping the dramatic bombshell on the eve of the Six Nations. In fact, Henry had delayed his statement out of concern for Howley and Cardiff Rugby Club. At the time Cardiff were fighting to qualify for the final stages of the European Cup, and Henry didn't want to distract Howley from the job in hand. He explained the situation to me: 'I didn't want to upset things for Cardiff. When I made my decision, Cardiff had some big games coming up in the Heineken Cup. I didn't want to affect their chances, so I withheld my announcement until after their match against Harlequins. Once that was out of the way and they had qualified, I felt free to make the change.' Howley was obviously upset by the decision, and there were worries that having the captaincy taken from him might affect his game adversely. However, he vowed to give 100 per cent for his new captain, and Graham was confident that the change would prompt Rob to achieve the status of the best scrum-half in the world.

Graham Henry had now been in charge for sixteen months, during which time he had enjoyed blanket support from the Welsh public and the media. Quite simply, Henry and his management team were beyond criticism. The first signs that this might be changing appeared in the build-up to the French match. Neath coach Lyn Jones went on record as saying that it was time for Henry to start making changes. Jones felt that Henry had taken the current group of international players as far as he could. It was time now to introduce some fresh blood. The problem with Jones's contention was that there were no new players who were obviously better than the current incumbents of the Welsh jersey. Having said that, I felt there was an element of truth in Jones's comment. However, making wholesale changes at this point could quite easily have undone much of the work of the past sixteen months. This team had transformed Welsh rugby. They were a side who had grown accustomed to winning, and they had moved us away from the black days when we lost games by fifty points. Henry could not afford to make changes that might jeopardise that transformation. I was certain that there would be changes during the international season, but they would come slowly. As it happened, the changes were forced on Henry at a pace which no one could have foreseen.

Further criticism came from Bob Dwyer, ex-coach of Australia and one of the most respected coaches in the world. Dwyer called the team's fitness into question. His comments were aimed at the squad in general, but he singled the Quinnell brothers out for particular attention. According to Dwyer, both of the Quinnells were badly overweight. In a television interview Dwyer said: 'I think the Quinnells could be fantastically good rugby players. But there aren't many great fat players on the international circuit.' The comment was, indirectly, a criticism of Steve Black's training methods, and Blackie immediately rallied to the defence of his players.

Scott Quinnell shrugged off the insult, claiming that his body fat was at an all-time low. If Dwyer had seen Scott playing, he might have reconsidered his judgement. I watched Scott play for Llanelli against Ebbw Vale in December and he was in awesome form. He came on as a substitute with Llanelli trailing to an impressive Ebbw outfit and made serious inroads into the home defence, before being sent off in a ridiculous incident, where he was deemed guilty of not releasing at a ruck. It was his first offence, but the third by a Llanelli player, so he was given his marching orders. As a result of this over-rigorous application of a new law, Ebbw Vale won a game which Quinnell had looked capable of winning for Llanelli. He was in impressive form again in the trial game at St Helens, and his weight certainly didn't appear to be slowing him up.

A more realistic appraisal of the situation came from within the Welsh camp. Shane Howarth is an experienced player who, despite adopting Welsh nationality, sees the game from an All Black perspective. He told me that he thought Wales were guilty of complacency. 'We've been living on the back of that winning run leading up to the World Cup,' he said. 'We have achieved so much, beating France, England and South Africa. The urgency and the daring that were evident against France in Paris were missing in our World Cup games. We were too conservative. We have to get back to taking people on, beating them with the ball in hand.' What Shane felt was missing from the Welsh team was the mental hardness which characterises the great All Black sides. This was exactly the trap which Graham had warned the players about before the Canadian game. Wales were no longer making it happen on the field – instead, they appeared to be waiting for things to happen, rather than dictating the game. Ironically, Howarth felt that one of Wales's weaknesses was their reliance on Neil Jenkins. 'Jenks is a great player, but we are relying on him too much,' he told me. 'Too often the game plan seems to be "get a penalty and Neil will put us in the game". We should be going for tries.'

Having enjoyed a ten-match winning run last year, Wales found themselves going into the Home Internationals having lost their last two games. Nobody underestimated the importance of this opening game. France were riding high as beaten finalists in the World Cup, and they brought a massive pack of forwards to Wales for the opening encounter of the international season. Wales needed to get back into their winning ways, and France were seen as possibly the strongest team in the tournament. Our main hope was that we would catch the French cold in their opening match.

Graham's plan was to take the game to the French and not

allow them to settle. The strategy was based around a simple and well-known fact about all French sides: they are good when things are going well, but don't react well to pressure. If you put them under pressure from the outset, they will lose their shape and their discipline. For the first twenty minutes everything went to plan – almost. Wales took the game to the French, and had them reeling. After thirteen minutes Jenkins put us ahead with a penalty. Five minutes later he missed with a similar kick, but the real indication that this was not to be our day was Wales's failure to take advantage of two clear-cut scoring opportunities. Dafydd James, not enjoying one of his better days, was involved in both incidents. First it seemed that he would score in the left corner, but as he tried to force his way over he lost possession and the ball went forward. Shortly after the Welsh penalty had put them ahead James received the ball, with Colin Charvis looping on his outside. He failed to find the wing forward and another chance went begging.

At this point the French had barely got out of their own half, but they obviously realised that the gods were with them and their confidence grew. Two penalties and a drop goal from Lamaison sent France into half-time with a 9–3 lead. The second half was all France. Olivier Magne and Thomas Castaignède scored superb tries, and scoring opportunities were missed again by Wales when Jones-Hughes and then Shane Howarth were held up on the French line. In reality Wales were never in it in the second half, and the loudest cheer of the half was reserved for the arrival of Shane Williams, coming on to win his first cap. Williams is the sort of player that the Welsh love: small but explosive. Unfortunately, it was no dream début for the little winger from Neath. His first significant act resulted in a try for Emile Ntamack. Williams was caught in the middle of a mazy run and tried to lay the ball off, only to see it snapped up by the French winger, who ran in the final French try. Luckily no blame was apportioned to the débutant, and I am sure that Williams will make a big contribution to the Welsh team in the years to come.

The final score of 36–3 represented Wales's worst performance yet under Graham Henry, but despite all the gloom which followed, things were not as bad as they seemed. Firstly, Scott Quinnell answered the criticisms of Bob Dwyer. He had an immense game, and was Wales's most effective attacking option. The players were definitely showing signs of fatigue, but despite that this was a game Wales could have won. I feel sure that had they taken those early chances, the result would have been very different. They lost because they failed to convert pressure into points.

Graham Henry refused to be panicked by the result. His feelings about the match were much the same as my own. He summed it up: 'In international football you have to take your opportunities. We blew those early chances. If you get the French down by fifteen points, it's a different game. It would have knocked France's confidence and put us in an excellent position.' However, the post-match analysis pointed to the fact that Henry would have to make changes for the next match, against tournament newcomers, Italy.

Italy were not expected to achieve a great deal in their first season in the Home International tournament, but they had already caused a major upset in defeating Scotland 34–20. With Welsh confidence having taken a knock against the French, the visit of the Italians to the Millennium Stadium was not quite the formality which had been expected. There were calls in the media for changes to the team – there was a feeling amongst many of the pundits that some of the seasoned internationals had peaked and that new blood was needed. In the bad old days there would probably have been wholesale changes, but Graham refused to hit the panic button. 'It may be that some complacency has crept into the side,' he said, 'but we don't have the strength in depth to consider changes galore.' Henry received support from his predecessor, Kevin Bowring, who confirmed that he thought Henry was taking Wales in the right direction, and warned against making too many changes.

However, there were rumblings of discontent from elsewhere. Following on from Bob Dwyer's comments about the Quinnell brothers, Peter Herbert of Llanelli and former Wales coach Alan Davies chipped in with queries about the training methods of Steve Black. They claimed that under Black's regime, players had put on weight and that their cardiovascular fitness had declined. Blackie insisted that he would stick by his methods, and that the stamina of the players was not in question. 'As an international team we need to be faster and sharper. We need to react quicker,' he said: 'Stamina work is not in question. I am trying to get an edge in other ways.'

I had had first-hand experience of Blackie's methods, and I was well aware that his approach was different to run-of-the-mill fitness coaches. As far as I was concerned he had been central to the success of the Welsh team through 1999, and I couldn't see that there were any grounds for the criticism. My assumption was that the matter would die down after a couple of good Welsh performances. I was aware from the time I spent talking to the players that they were close to exhaustion and that the only cure for this was some time away from the game.

Graham made changes to the side before Wales faced Italy. Allan Bateman and Craig Quinnell had missed the French match through injury. They were now fit, and were duly reinstated. Shane Williams had done enough on his début to claim the wing berth ahead of Dafydd James, and Geraint Lewis came in on the blind side in place of Colin Charvis. Not the wholesale changes that some had called for, but generally these were accepted as wise selections.

One of the criticisms of the Welsh team in recent games had been that we were becoming one-dimensional and predictable. Bateman's selection went some way to combating that. Allan is a consummate footballer. His vision and experience enable him to turn a match and break the toughest of defences. Williams brought sheer pace to the wing. Geraint Lewis is a footballing back-row man who would give Wales more pace and variety than Charvis could offer. The return of the younger Quinnell was also welcome, and it must have been pleasing to Craig to see his critics answered. Scott had played magnificently against France, but too often he had been the only ball-carrier. With his brother in the team, Wales had two powerhouses capable of punching through the Italian defence.

Against Scotland the Argentinian transplant Diego Dominguez had kicked Italy to victory. At Cardiff, it was Neil Jenkins's turn to pick up the points. The kicking machine put over seven penalties and three conversions to push Wales to a convincing victory, by 47 points to 16. In the first half Wales were really back on song.

Shane Williams took to international football with vigorous ease. He was full of confidence, and his fizz and spark were rewarded with a first international try. In response the crowd took him to their hearts – every time he touched the ball they were on their feet in anticipation. Scott Quinnell had another great game, and was rewarded with a try. Further tries from Allan Bateman and Shane Howarth rounded out the Welsh score. Wales dominated the first two-thirds of the game, but with the job done they went off the boil and allowed Italy to keep the score respectable. This led to further comments on the fitness levels of the team. Graham, quite rightly, refused to be drawn on this particular subject. 'It's a bit of a hobby for people to get on that bandwagon,' he told the post-match press conference. 'The best thing is to ignore it. We don't have a problem in that department.' He knew where the problem lay: not in the training methods of Steve Black, but in the gruelling schedule that the players had followed for the past two years. However, the media had got its teeth into this particular bone

THE DRAGON AWAKES

and they were determined to chew it over at length. The issue was not going to be put to bed for some time.

Everybody was pleased by the result against Italy, but the comment that always followed any discussion of the game went along the lines that it was a good result, but against a poor side, and that England would be a different proposition.

Having defeated France in Paris, England were now firm favourites for the championship. They were also still rankling about their defeat at Wembley a year earlier. Wales's record at Twickenham in recent seasons was lamentable. Both of these factors indicated the prospect of an extremely tough visit.

In Wales, the England game is huge. I have not experienced such hype for any other sporting event; the game dominates the sporting media for a week before the big day. The pressure on the players is immense. The squad training sessions are watched by fans and press, and every action is scrutinised. Talking to Graham during the build-up to the game, he told me: 'This is a must-win game. I mean, they're all must-win games, but this one is special. This is the one game each year that everyone wants to win. In the national psyche, it's more important than all the others. The expectation of the Welsh public is immense.'

Graham tried to lessen the pressure on his players by holding training sessions behind closed doors. My feeling was that they were drained and would struggle against a powerful, and fresher, England team. Most of the leading English players had enjoyed a summer's rest, and as a result were in better shape than the Welsh. I felt that part of Graham's reasoning in holding the training sessions in purdah was to avoid letting anyone know just how tired his troops were.

When we spoke on the Wednesday before the match, Graham went through the game plan with me and talked up our chances, but he also gave me an insight into his worries for the team. 'Basically,' he said, 'we are treading water. We are not making any progress, and we won't make progress until the guys have a break. They're struggling to get that edge because they've played too much rugby. They're buggered. If we play to our potential, we've got a chance – hopefully, the occasion will bring it out.' His game plan was fairly simple, but it relied on our forwards holding parity with the English pack in the tight and in the loose, for the full eighty minutes. The aim was to play for field position; England would be doing the same. When attacking the English line, the intention had to be to get the ball wide to Shane Williams and Gareth Thomas, our most potent attacking weapons.

Graham had great respect for the English, especially in defence: 'The English defence is very strong,' he told me. 'They stack their defence in midfield. If they have a weakness, it is out wide. We have the players who can exploit that weakness, if we can get the ball out to the wide channel.' This was the first time I had felt that Graham was talking a good game without really believing it.

On my way out of the team hotel I ran into Chris Wyatt, and my chat with him confirmed my worst fears. I had spent quite a bit of time with Chris in the past year. He is one of the team characters, and is always very upbeat. His manner is very laid back and friendly and he is always up for anything. On this occasion, though, he was very subdued, and looked wrecked. If he was any kind of indicator, the boys would not be going into this game with a full tank.

Saturday came around, and as I prepared myself for the match my mind returned to the tired figure I had spoken to on Wednesday, and to the words of Graham Henry. The only cause for optimism was the thought that, as Graham had said, the occasion might bring out the best in the team. I was not confident.

In the opening phases of the game, Wales more than held their own. The Welsh front row gave England a torrid time at the scrum, and Chris Wyatt showed what a great lineout jumper he is by stealing balls from Greening's throws. Jenkins kicked his usual brace of penalties and dropped a goal. But I felt the writing was on the wall very early on. England were playing the game at pace, and appeared determined to play fifteen-man rugby in a fast and loose fashion. That they were capable of doing this was illustrated by the work of their hooker, Phil Greening. He was everywhere, and so at ease with the ball in his hands. Greening was rewarded for his skills by scoring the opening try of the game from thirty-five yards out.

At half-time Wales were only trailing by seven points, but they had been chasing the game and I knew this would take its toll on them in the second half. It was obvious to me that we couldn't keep up with the pace, and that something would crack. England proved me right, big time. They dominated the second half completely, scoring twenty-seven points without reply. True, they were playing against a jaded side, depleted by the sin-binning of Scott Quinnell and Garin Jenkins, but to give credit where it is due, they were playing superb rugby. Forwards and backs were almost indistinguishable. Greening continued to shine, and Dallaglio furthered his claim to being the best back-row forward in the modern game. Dallaglio, Back and Hill all scored tries, before allowing Cohen to get one for the backs. Wales were simply blown away. They lost their shape and their discipline, and were playing the game in a different time to the English.

In the second half England were the epitome of the modern rugby team, while Wales were cumbersome and laboured. The final score was 46–12, and Wales were lucky to have kept the margin as tight as that. The difference in points was the same as the last time the two sides had met at Twickenham, and on that occasion the result had precipitated the demise of the Welsh coach. Henry's position was still secure, but as a result of this game the pressure was most definitely mounting for some kind of change.

NINE

THE GLOVES ARE OFF

THE KNIVES WERE MOST DEFINITELY OUT following the England game. Criticism of the team poured in from the public, the press and a host of former internationals, all of whom had their own pet theory as to why we had lost. Former stars such as Barry John, J.J. Williams and Bobby Windsor fuelled the flames with comments about Wales's humiliation and being embarrassed to be Welsh.

The alacrity with which the supposed supporters of the national team leapt on the bandwagon surprised and saddened me. I remembered a conversation in the bar of the team hotel in Gatwick on the eve of our trip to Portugal. The management team were having a quiet drink before retiring for the night when Trevor James made the assertion that a significant number of people in Wales wanted the team to do badly. I responded that, in my experience, the fans were right behind the team and only wanted them to do well. James insisted that there was a culture of envy which meant that a large number of people involved in the game relished the opportunity to stick the knife in when things were going badly. 'There is no mileage for them,' he reiterated, 'when the Welsh team is rolling along smoothly.' Now, in early March, his words echoed prophetically.

The Dragon Awakes

I was sickened by the treatment the players and the Welsh management received at this time. The ex-internationals, in particular, seemed to take a superficial and unconstructive approach to the situation. Nobody epitomised the mindless attitude of 'things were different in my day' more than Bobby Windsor. Windsor was a great player in his time, but his time was far removed from the current state of the game. His perceptive analysis in *The Western Mail*, was that the players were playing too little rugby. They should, he said, 'Spend more time playing and less time being lovey-dovey and having rubdowns.' How's that for clear, clinical analysis? The reaction of these stars made *me* embarrassed to be Welsh!

There was a huge overreaction to the English defeat. This stemmed in part from unrealistic expectations on the part of the Welsh supporters, fuelled by the media, who then used them to attack the team in their time of crisis. The scenario followed a familiar pattern which goes something like this: Wales win a couple of games and are lauded as world-beaters. They then lose a match and are denigrated as unfit, unprofessional and unworthy to represent Wales. This is invariably followed by demands for wholesale changes in the playing and coaching staff. The press and a significant number of supporters complained about the way we lost to England – a more positive approach would have been to acknowledge how well England had played. In these circumstances, in the eyes of the critics, a game is never won by the opposition, but is lost by Wales. The fact is that England played superbly, and on that form would have pushed even the best of international sides.

In the wake of that defeat, the very people who had claimed that Graham Henry was the Great Redeemer now dubbed him a false Messiah. Their hyperbolic reaction prompted many level-headed rugby fans to suggest that Henry might up sticks and return to New Zealand. We have seen this treatment meted out to successive Welsh coaches, and many thought that Henry couldn't be blamed if he just packed it all in. Fortunately for us, his pragmatic approach means that, while I am sure he doesn't enjoy such criticism, he lets it wash over him. He was bemused but unaffected by the Great Redeemer tag, and took the adverse criticism in the same vein. Unlike the Welsh public, Henry had never expected to turn Wales into world-beaters overnight. We had enjoyed several highs in the last year, beating France in Paris, nicking the game from under the English noses at Wembley and defeating world champions South Africa, but losing to England had rocked us right back. The wheel, it seemed, had turned full circle.

To misquote an old saying, when one door closes, another one slams in your face. Just when we thought things had reached an all-time low, events took yet another turn for the worse. Even the phlegmatic Welsh coach must have despaired at the events which unfolded in the build-up to the Scotland game.

There had always been disquiet in some quarters over Henry's imports. The importation of Welsh Kiwis and Aussies was criticised by some on the grounds that it was at the expense of home-grown talent. In fact, the paucity of home-produced skills had prompted Graham to look abroad for a quick fix solution to some of our problems. The joke went around that whatever your origins, you could play for Wales if your family had ever enjoyed a weekend in Rhyl. This joke backfired when it was revealed that Brett Sinkinson, the New Zealand-born Neath flanker, had no Welsh antecedents and was therefore not eligible to play for Wales. Sinkinson had been an integral member of the team that had enjoyed an unbeaten ten-match run in 1999. A report in a Scottish newspaper claimed that Sinkinson's grandfather was English, not Welsh. The report also cast doubt over the eligibility of Shane Howarth, and it was announced that until the matter was sorted out, Howarth would not be considered for selection for the Welsh team. He was duly omitted from the side to play Scotland.

The Dragon Awakes

The disquiet in the media turned into a feeding frenzy and every pundit who had ever questioned the advisability of playing foreign-born players hastily adopted an 'I told you so' stance. The credentials of all the imported players were put under scrutiny. David Pickering issued an official statement saying, 'The WRU has decided to examine, once again, the credentials of all players who wish to play for Wales.' He insisted that the union had always followed the standard practice in accepting proof of eligibility. 'In the recent cases of Shane Howarth, Brett Sinkinson, Jason Jones-Hughes and Matt Cardey, the players followed the accepted practice of all nations by writing to the governing body to register their claim for selection. Once it was established that they had a qualification, their names were put forward to the national team management for consideration.'

Matt Cardey hurriedly obtained a copy of his grandmother's birth certificate, showing her to have been born in Nantyglo, and thus verifying his claim for selection against Scotland. Sinkinson's claim to Welshness seemed hopeless. Sidney Sinkinson, it appeared, had lived in Wales prior to his departure for New Zealand, but he was unquestionably English.

Howarth remained in limbo. He stuck to his claim that his maternal grandfather was a Thomas Williams of Cardiff. Howarth had a sworn affidavit from his mother, stating that his grandfather was from Cardiff. However, a birth certificate showed that his grandfather was Hare Matenga Wirema, a Maori from Opoha, New Zealand. There was an implication that there was some family history which Howarth, understandably, didn't want to discuss in public. Howarth is a strong family man who dotes on his young son, and he clearly felt that these issues were private. He was evidently upset by the whole affair, and there was a lot of sympathy and support for him amongst the Welsh public. Howarth was the highest-profile of the 'imported' players in Graham Henry's team, and he was, and is, hugely popular with the Welsh fans. He always gave 100 per cent every time he pulled on a Welsh jersey, and his pride in playing for Wales was evident every time he lined up for the national anthem. As he says, he feels at home in Wales, and, whatever the IRB says, he considers himself Welsh. As it became obvious that he couldn't verify his claim to eligibility, and his place in the team passed to Matt Cardey he vowed that he would do everything in his power to win back his place after he had qualified on residential grounds. As far as I am concerned, if Shane Howarth tells me he's Welsh, he's Welsh.

In the light of the numerous cases of foreign nationals playing for adopted countries, I think that Sinkinson and Howarth were treated very badly. For the other players in the squad, however much sympathy they felt for their colleagues, the game had to go on and so they prepared for the Scottish match. The team closed ranks and went into purdah, training behind closed doors and limiting public comments to a minimum. The atmosphere within the camp soon became tense and strained.

The enforced absence of Sinkinson and Howarth, along with injuries to Jenkins and Scott Quinnell, forced Henry to announce a much-altered side to face Scotland. There were eight changes in all, including the axing of Robert Howley. Howley had never recaptured the form he enjoyed prior to the Lions' tour to South Africa, and the fact that his star was on the wane was illustrated by his losing the captaincy at the start of the season. An overdose of rugby and worries over the health of his baby daughter had taken their toll on the scrum-half, and his performances were laborious and jaded. I felt that the choice of Rupert Moon as his replacement was an indication that Graham saw this loss of form as only a temporary phenomenon. Howley is a world-class player and is therefore central to the development of the Welsh team.

The selection of the experienced Moon as his replacement was very much a case of 'horses for courses'. I could see the logic in it: Moon was an experienced player, and he would be playing alongside his Llanelli teammate, outside-half Stephen Jones. However, I must admit I would have preferred to have seen Richard Smith brought in to replace Howley, as Moon's selection was a short-term move, and offered nothing for the future development of the team. Also, I felt that while Moon would bring enthusiasm and a huge presence to the game, Smith was a better all-round player.

The tribal element within me was pleased to see Ebbw Vale's Nathan Budgett rewarded for some awesome performances at club and A team level by selection in the starting line-up, and by the presence of Smith and Jason Strange on the bench. On the other hand, I was saddened to see Sinkinson and Howarth discarded after such laudable service in the Welsh cause. If they are not Welsh, they should be given honorary citizenship! I felt they were badly treated throughout the whole affair. I had spent time with both men during the last year, and know them to be honest and straightforward. I am certain that both of them were convinced of their eligibility to play for Wales, and there was no question of them trying to hoodwink anyone. OK, they were vague about where their grandparents had come from – I know I couldn't tell you where *my* grandfather was born. They had simply accepted family lore about their ancestors.

The onus, I feel, is on the respective rugby unions to validate claims of nationality, and the buck, as far as I am concerned, stops with the WRU. There was talk of an amnesty for the players, which would have been fair. The rules on eligibility were vague and poorly policed. This was the fault of the unions involved, not the players. If the union had been doing its job properly, the discrepancy would have been discovered before the players were selected for Wales. A disciplinary tribunal, convened by the IRB in Dublin, decided that no further action would be taken against either the WRU or the players concerned. The WRU, together with the SRU, who were also in the dock concerning the selection of the Bristol-born prop

David Hilton, had to pay costs, but otherwise the issue was to be considered closed. Howarth and Sinkinson were punished by the curtailing of their international careers, yet the unions, who were ultimately responsible for the entire fiasco, got off scot-free. Phil Kingsley-Jones, who had been responsible for Sinkinson signing for Neath, summed it up by saying, 'The players have been hung out to dry and made scapegoats for the union.'

Unfortunately, as with the confusion over ticket sales for the World Cup, this was another example of rugby as a professional game being run by amateurs. This is an issue which needs to be addressed. Certainly the New Zealand Rugby Union appears to have driven a coach and horses through the regulations, as Samoans seem to transfer, almost at will, between the New Zealand and Samoan teams.

The issue of eligibility is one which will run and run and it is obvious that the International Rugby Board must do something to clarify the situation. The cases of Howarth and Sinkinson were clearly genuine mistakes which might have been avoided had the union made more of an effort to verify their claims to Welsh nationality. However, the muddled nature of the laws was highlighted by the announcement that Nick Walne, the Cardiff winger, was also ineligible to play for Wales. Walne was born in England but had lived in Wales since he was six. He had attended university in England and then joined Richmond Rugby Club. He had only just returned to Wales when he won his first cap. His only claim to Welsh nationality was one of residency, and as he had not been resident in Wales for thirty-six months prior to his selection, he was deemed ineligible. Walne had represented Wales at all junior levels, and clearly considered himself to be Welsh. The IRB regulations evidently had no contingency plans to cover such a case.

Howarth and Sinkinson were in the limelight as the high-profile players involved, but other players were proved to be ineligible, notably David Hilton of Scotland. I am sure other cases will arise, unless the IRB tightens up the regulations and makes them more intelligible. The whole issue was very distressing for the players involved, and was a distraction from the main event. Howarth and Sinkinson will be in the limelight until another case arises. As Saturday approached, the immediate question for the Welsh was how the team would react in the face of such adversity.

The new-look Welsh team, containing, ironically, five players born outside Wales, took the field against Scotland, knowing that a defeat now would bring the whole Graham Henry road-show to a shuddering halt. Graham appeared decidedly tense and drawn throughout the build-up to the game. There was even speculation in the press that Henry might be about to quit. He had an opt-out clause in his contract with the WRU, and many thought that he was close to invoking it. Neil Jenkins came out in support of the coach, saying that without him Welsh rugby would return to the dark ages. Graham tried to put an end to the rumours by declaring publicly that he was staying. 'I am not going to be chucking it in,' he told the Welsh press, 'but everybody involved has to be disciplined enough to get back to where we were a year ago, and that means there has to be a big improvement against Scotland. I said last year that there was too much hype surrounding the victories we enjoyed and the same is true now, after a poor start to the championship. It seems that there is either total elation in Wales or utter despair. There is no middle ground, no sense of perspective, and it has an unsettling effect.'

If the pressure on the national coach was mounting, it was nothing compared to the growing disquiet over the role of Steve Black. The perception of a growing number of pundits and supporters was that we had lost to England because of their superior fitness. Paul Thorburn, former captain of Wales and Director of the Rugby World Cup, was the latest to join the fray. Thorburn seemed to relish the opportunity to join the pack of ex-players sticking the knife into the current incumbents of the Welsh shirt. His criticism revolved, predictably, around the lack of dedication on the part of the Welsh players, and the failure of the management to enforce a disciplined fitness regime. Perhaps the management should offer these pundits the opportunity to attend a few training sessions in order to see the work rate for themselves. In all the time that I spent in weights rooms with members of the Welsh squad, I don't recall seeing a single member of the press.

Rob Howley tried to give the other side of the story, pointing out that he had been on summer tours every year since 1996 and that last summer, while Wales were preparing for internationals against South Africa, France and Canada, the English were training at a sports resort in Australia. It is crucial that players build reserves of fitness during the summer. They can then start the season with a full tank, which will, hopefully, see them through to the end of the year. In recent years, the Welsh players had been unable to take the recovery time needed to recharge their batteries. As Graham had told me, they wouldn't improve until they had some serious rest. Howley emphasised the level of support for Black amongst the players, and stressed the importance of his role in the improved fortunes of the Welsh team in 1999.

It was clear to those closest to the action that the management team were doing everything that was possible to control the current decline in form. Both Henry and Black enjoyed the complete confidence of the players. However, it was clear that whatever might be said by those directly involved, a win against Scotland was imperative. The conditions in the build-up to the game were obviously far from ideal. The squad felt the pressure of the nation on their backs. The eligibility scandal was, at the very least, a distraction. It had also relieved Henry of the services of two of his key players. Injuries to others, including Scott Quinnell and Neil Jenkins, enforced further changes. As the

THE DRAGON AWAKES

match day approached, returning scrum-half Rupert Moon likened the siege mentality to that of Rorke's Drift, and claimed that this would turn to Wales's advantage as they closed ranks against Scotland. While everybody understood the allusion, nobody had the heart to point out what had happened to the Welsh on that particular occasion.

The reputations of the two Welsh coaches were on the line going into this match. Wales won a scrappy match, which I assumed might be enough to stop the criticism of Henry and Black. The press were distracted by their burgeoning love affair with the diminutive winger from Neath. Shane Williams's star was most definitely in the ascendancy.

Scotland were having a nightmare season, which began with their historic defeat at the hands of the Italians. As they approached the Welsh game they were looking squarely down the barrel of a Six Nations whitewash. The pressure that both sides were under was hardly conducive to either of them playing confident, flowing, attacking rugby, and the match was in truth a poor spectacle. Wales won, but only just, and my feeling was that they had been the better of two poor sides on the day. However, there were bright points, most notably the performance of Williams. He appeared blithely unaware of the stresses which seemed to be burdening everyone else on the pitch, playing with joyous verve and abandon. He scored two excellent tries, and ran the ball at every opportunity.

Another ray of hope was the performance of Stephen Jones. Jones seems to me to have been around for years. In fact, he is only twenty-two, but he played in this match with an assurance that belies his years and relative lack of experience. He ran the line with confidence and varied his game excellently. Jones is closer to the typical Welsh outside-half than Jenkins is, and with this performance he finally established himself in the international arena. He was obviously helped by the presence of his club scrum-half, Rupert Moon. Moon showed some technical deficiencies, but compensated for these by chivvying the forwards into action all afternoon. Amongst the forwards, I felt Budgett and Gough were outstanding. Matt Cardey, a New Zealander of proven Welsh descent, started shakily, but soon settled down to enjoy an excellent début.

The defence by all the Welsh players was awesome – they held their shape and put in an enormous number of hits. The defensive requirements were an indication of just how much ball the Scots got. Ian McGeechan must have been tearing his hair out at the profligacy of his players, and the Scots definitely squandered possession and scoring opportunities. A victory of 26–18 may not be all that convincing, but on occasions like that a win is a win. The heat was off Graham and his team, and it appeared that for once his major problem, looking forward to the Irish game, was whether to stick to his winning team or to bring back some of the older players who had now recovered from injuries.

In fact, the feel-good factor created by the Scottish win lasted about twenty-four hours. On the Sunday after the Scottish match, I was driving back from lunch in the Vale of Glamorgan. It was a beautiful day, I had enjoyed an excellent lunch, and generally life was running pretty smoothly. Until I turned on the radio to hear the news. The lead sports story concerned the resignation of Wales's fitness coach, Steve Black. I couldn't believe it. I knew that Blackie had been getting a lot of stick from the media, but I had hoped we'd heard the last of that after the previous day's victory. In a formal press release, Lyn Davies, the WRU media manager, explained: 'Following a period of unprecedented attack from some sections of the media on his professional integrity, competence and commitment, Mr Black is not prepared to expose either himself or his family to further public vilification.'

In addition to the witch hunt concerning the fitness of the Welsh squad, one newspaper had got hold of the story that

THE DRAGON AWAKES

Blackie was doing a bit of fitness coaching at Fulham football club. The accusation was that Black wasn't committed to the Welsh cause, and that he should have been working with our international players instead of giving his time to London footballers. Apparently Blackie's children were getting a lot of abuse at school, and it was this that prompted him to resign. I know that Graham Henry and the management team did everything they could to dissuade him, but when the malicious smear campaign started to affect his family, Black obviously felt he had no choice but to protect them by resigning.

I was really saddened by the whole affair. Blackie is a lovely bloke and really didn't deserve this treatment. Anyone who'd had anything to do with him knew that his commitment to his work was total. No one could do more for the Welsh players than Blackie, and they all knew that he was there for them twenty-four hours a day. David Young spoke for all the players when he said that he was bitter about the way Blackie had been treated. The players who had worked with him over the previous eighteen months all knew exactly how important the role he had played in the revival of Welsh fortunes was. My feeling during that wonderful winning streak in 1999 was that Black was just as important as Graham Henry in transforming the side. He was an integral member of the set-up, and I felt he was crucial to the continuing development of the squad. He would certainly be missed, and the Welsh squad was weaker for his departure. But my main feeling was one of anger that such a fine man should be treated so shabbily.

Blackie's methods are undoubtedly unconventional, and he is much more than simply a fitness adviser. His system is holistic; he deals with the needs of each individual player. He is concerned with both the physical and psychological well-being of his charges. He knows the weaknesses of all the players, but he also knows their strengths and their aspirations and sees his job as creating an environment where they can realise these aspirations. He did as much as anyone to create an atmosphere of self-belief and self-confidence in the Welsh camp. His methods were central to the building of the successful Welsh side. These methods didn't suddenly become outmoded or invalid as Wales's form declined; there were other factors involved.

I think Graham Henry and Black would admit that some of the players had become complacent, but for the most part they were simply worn out. They had nothing left to give. In addition to this, there must have been a huge feeling of anti-climax following the World Cup. The players were simply not capable, emotionally or physically, of gearing themselves up for yet another round of international matches. Blackie's enforced resignation evidently hit the team hard, and there was much anger amongst the players and the management at the way the coach had been treated. Graham Henry stuck by his friend and paid fulsome tribute to his ability, 'Steve Black is a one-off. He is a marvellous person. He had a hugely positive relationship with the team. He is one of the leading fitness coaches in the world, and his commitment was total. What has happened is completely unfair. It is disappointing that people cannot see what a top person we had in the job.' He concluded that those who had forced Black out would rue the day that they had driven him to resign.

The Welsh management could have been forgiven for harbouring feelings of paranoia, as their problems seemed to multiply daily. At first it had been the relatively straightforward worry over performances, but to this had been added the debate about the eligibility of Graham Henry's imported players. Now we had the resignation of a key member of the management team. As if all of this wasn't enough, there was suddenly a question over the WRU's financial arrangements for the Rugby World Cup. There seemed to be a shortfall of some £17 million in the monies paid to Rugby World Cup Ltd by the WRU.

The Dragon Awakes

This situation was hardly creating an environment for producing a winning rugby team. However, Wales had one match remaining, Ireland away, and Graham Henry had to distance himself from all the distractions and concentrate on beating the Irish. The Scottish result had been a good one, but everybody was aware that the Scottish team had been poor, and we would need to perform better to defeat the Irish in Lansdowne Road.

When Graham announced the line-up for the Irish game, there were a few changes in the team that had defeated Scotland. The talismanic Scott Gibbs returned for the injured Mark Taylor. Matt Cardey was unlucky to miss out through injury, after an excellent début against Scotland. His place was taken by the young Cardiff full-back, Rhys Williams. Apart from these forced changes, Graham stuck with the side that had won against Scotland. There were some grounds for confidence on the part of the Welsh team. Perversely, this fixture seems to favour the away side, and Wales have won seven of their last nine matches in the Irish capital.

The Scottish match had been played under intense pressure, and this had undoubtedly affected the quality of the play. The situation eased a little in time for the Irish game, and the players seemed more confident and relaxed. Once again, this was a game of two halves. Wales dominated the first half and went in at half-time leading 10–6, only to fall away in the second half and allow the Irish back into the match. That said, it was a good performance by Wales: the Irish threw everything at us in the second half, and the boys played with determination and grit. Once again, there was a feeling that whatever happened we would stick in there and win the day. Eventually, the *coup de grâce* was delivered by Neil Jenkins, who came on with fifteen minutes left and Wales trailing 19–17. His first act on entering the field was to put over a penalty to push Wales ahead. A second kick put us further ahead, but the game wasn't safe until the final whistle blew.

THE DRAGON AWAKES

The 23–19 victory was not exactly an emphatic one, but there were plenty of plus points for Wales. Our front row dominated their Irish opponents completely. David Young, Garin Jenkins and Peter Rogers had performed consistently in the tight all season, and must now be confident in standing up to any opposition. Our back row also played well. Geraint Lewis brought superb footballing skills to the mix, and Nathan Budgett has proved to be quite a find. In addition to his superb work in the loose, he offers Wales another option at the tail of the lineout. Stephen Jones had another impressive game, as did Shane Williams. However, this game really belonged to Rhys Williams. I had been impressed with Rhys when we first met in Portugal, and had been further impressed by his performances for Cardiff. In this game he really shone. He showed inventiveness and daring and, like Shane Williams, he has sheer, dazzling pace. On a number of occasions he made thirty-yard breaks, leaving a trail of Irish players in his wake.

It was significant that the players singled out for praise were, for the most part, newcomers. True, players like Stephen Jones and Geraint Lewis had been on the fringes of the team for some time, but this was the first time they had really competed to make their positions their own. Suddenly, it seemed, there was real competition for places. Graham Henry was evidently pleased by the way the season had finished, and I think he may even have been a little surprised at how well the new players had adapted to the rigours of international football. 'We have blooded a number of untried players, and we've discovered that we have a lot more in reserve than we thought,' he said. 'A number of these players are new to international football, but you wouldn't have guessed it from the way they played today.'

Victory over Ireland left Wales in fourth place in the Six Nations Championship, level on points with Ireland and France. As is often the case, the championship table masked the real relative strengths of the competitors. England were deservedly

The Dragon Awakes

the champions, and only missed out on a Grand Slam thanks to an inexplicable loss to Scotland at Murrayfield. Quite how England managed to blow it yet again is beyond most people, but their ability to do all the hard work only to fall at the apparently simple final hurdle, is one of the wonders of modern rugby. It is also a source of huge enjoyment to all the Celtic nations. Long may it continue!

France must have been disappointed by their season, especially after reaching the final of the World Cup. Before the tournament started, England and France were clear favourites to win the championship. Their defeat 27–25, at the hands of the Irish, in Paris, was as surprising as England losing to Scotland. Both results show the unpredictability of the game and illustrate the enduring appeal of the championship. None of the sides in the tournament is so strong that success is guaranteed. In fact, had Ireland managed to overcome Wales at Lansdowne Road, they would have had a share in the championship. Ireland were completely unfancied at the beginning of the tournament, but their season was made by the win in Paris.

Scotland's season was little short of disastrous, but the hurt was no doubt eased by their victory over England. Italy, the newcomers, probably did better than they could have expected. Their win against Scotland was totally unexpected, and should give them heart for the future. For Wales, the results were much as expected and from that point of view the season was a disappointment. However, this was not a normal year. The rigours of the World Cup took their toll, and resulted in the team underperforming in most matches.

So, Graham Henry's second season as Welsh coach drew to a close. The season had been a long and arduous one. Possibly it had also been disappointing, but this may have been because our expectations had been too high. Crucially, the season had ended on a high note. We had unearthed a new generation of star players. They will, hopefully, take the game on a further step or two. Interestingly, they will be the first complete professionals. The people who have been playing for Wales for the past five years are all players who grew up and learnt their rugby under the amateur ethos. They have had to adapt their habits and behaviour to suit the rigours of the new professional game. Many of them have adapted very well, but it has required a huge cultural transformation. The new generation consists of people who never knew the old amateur game. They have come into the sport aware of the needs of professionalism from day one.

Currently, the young stars are wowing the crowds with their verve and vigour, their evident joy at playing international rugby. However, they are only just starting on the treadmill. The game's organisers must be careful not to run them into the ground. The cycle goes round pretty quickly now. I hope that Shane and Rhys Williams continue to enjoy the kind of success they had at the end of last season. If they do, they could find themselves off to Australia in the summer of 2001 to play for the Lions. After that, there will be another international season at home, and by that time we will be preparing for the World Cup once again. It is easy for the most enthusiastic player to become jaded.

At the close of the 1999–2000 season, the old hands were to be given a well-earned rest over the summer, while the youngsters went on a development tour of Canada. Graham was going on the Canadian tour as an observer, but he was keen to stress that he saw it as crucial. He was hoping to find half a dozen youngsters who would compete for a place in the national team next season. After the emotional stress of the past six months, Graham might have been hoping for a bit of time to relax over the summer. Some hope!

TEN

THE WAY FORWARD

GRAHAM HENRY ARRIVED IN WALES to a fanfare welcome and rapidly established himself as the saviour of the national game. He himself had certainly never encouraged the hype that surrounded his arrival. He was slightly bemused by the furore, and by the way he was cast as the Great Redeemer. Graham had never underestimated the task before him, never claimed that he could turn the team around overnight. Unfortunately for him, a great number of the Welsh public did believe just that. Their expectations were unrealistically high.

The honeymoon period between Graham and the Welsh public and media lasted longer than anyone should reasonably have expected. In fact, despite a few bumpy moments, Graham has had a pretty easy ride in this respect, and his stock is still very high throughout the country. The mixed nature of the results has made it hard for people to clearly understand his achievements. There have been the obvious highs of wins over France, England and South Africa, but these have been balanced by a number of lows, notably England and France this season. Despite the low points Graham Henry has, I feel, transformed the Welsh team during his first two years, from a side that routinely lost to the leading nations by near-cricket scores to a team who are able to compete, at least, with the world's best.

On his arrival, Henry complained that the side played in too pedestrian a manner. His first job was to develop a side which could play at pace. During their ten-match winning sequence, Wales achieved this pace, most notably against France in Paris and again against South Africa in Cardiff. The work of Steve Black was central to this transformation. Another factor in the change was the restructured Welsh–Scottish League.

When Henry first arrived, there was much talk of developing four super-teams. This caused much dissent amongst Welsh supporters, who saw the possibility of unfashionable clubs, such as Ebbw Vale and Pontypridd, being sacrificed to the greater good of the game in Wales. Henry underestimated the tribal nature of the game in the Principality. The 1999–2000 season ended with six sides competing for the championship, and a resultant increased pool of players from which Henry could draw for the national side.

As the season drew to a close, he acknowledged that things had improved but believed that there was still room for improvement. 'The situation with regard to strength in depth has improved dramatically,' he told me. 'There is better strength and the situation is more even, but we are still lacking the superstars. You need a few of those, and there are a number of players about whom I am optimistic. Hopefully, the development tour will bring them out. This tour is important. We need competition for places. Until recently we have not had that. The team was picking itself until the last couple of games last year.'

By the end of the inaugural Six Nations tournament team selection was less automatic. Nathan Budgett, Geraint Lewis and Ian Gough were all vying for permanent places in the first team and there was also competition amongst the half-backs – all of which added to the mood of optimism evident at the end of the season. This optimism was vested in the two young men who, more than any others, had come to symbolise the future of Welsh rugby, Shane and Rhys Williams. Both players have genuine pace. More importantly, they have the spark of genius about them. They are prepared to take risks and make things happen. Both made impressive starts to their international careers. Last season they enjoyed the benefit of being unknown, but next season both will be marked men and will find life much harder. In their second season, they will find that the gaps get smaller and they will be given more attention by opposition defences. It is to be hoped that the Welsh public and media will continue to support them and not give them the kind of rollercoaster ride that other players, such as Neil Jenkins, have endured during their time in the team.

After two years of ceaseless activity, the senior players were rested over the summer and hopefully they will start the new season refreshed, with full tanks. Over the summer, the younger players took part in a development tour of Canada. Henry's hope was that this tour would throw up new faces who would compete for places in the national team in the coming season. The tour was an unqualified success, and there will be serious competition for places in the autumn internationals against the USA, Samoa and South Africa.

After the trials and tribulations of the 1999–2000 season, the Canadian tour gave Graham Henry some breathing space and represented a positive start to the next phase in the development of the national game. Henry's appointment as coach to the British Lions for their forthcoming tour of Australia was another plus, although it has added to his already prodigious workload. He was scheduled to accompany the development tour to Canada as an observer, and was probably looking forward to a more relaxing tour than he is accustomed to. In the event, he had to fly back and forth between the UK and Canada to finalise his appointment as the Lions' coach.

The Dragon Awakes

Once the Canadian tour was over, Henry spent time in Australia and South Africa watching the Tri-Nations tournament, in preparation for next summer's Tests against Australia. Presumably, the research programme on his Lions' opponents is well underway and the video player in the Henry household is working overtime. His selection as Lions' coach represents a huge vote of confidence in Henry, and it can only strengthen his hand as he pushes for the necessary changes in the structure of the game in Wales, and the UK in general. Hopefully, a successful Lions tour to Australia will focus the attention of all concerned towards strengthening the game in the Northern Hemisphere.

Looking towards the new season, it is to be hoped that the Welsh–Scottish League will provide still more meaningful competition. The two Scottish district sides were uncompetitive last year, but they appear stronger this year. The Welsh clubs should also be stronger. Cardiff, Swansea, Newport and Llanelli will, predictably, lead the challenge. In recent years Pontypridd and Ebbw Vale have built up enviable reputations, and both are notoriously difficult to beat on their home grounds. This should prove to be the case again. Neath emerged as a strong side at the end of the last campaign. They have a number of exciting young backs, allied to some experienced forwards, and should be a force to reckon with in the coming season. Bridgend have made some useful acquisitions during the close season, and with Dennis John at the helm they should now be competitive.

With ten well-balanced sides in the league, prospective internationals will be playing in hard-fought games on a regular basis. The gulf between the established sides and the newcomers, such as Caerphilly and Cross Keys, is becoming uncrossable. Caerphilly are beginning to come to terms with life in the Premiership, but I doubt that Cross Keys will have time to become established. I wish them well – they have played some attractive rugby and getting into the top echelon of the game is a real achievement – but I cannot help feeling sorry for them. Try as they might, their players face the prospect of a forty- or fifty-point drubbing every time they play in the league. This cannot do anything for the confidence of the players, and it does nothing to improve the image of the league.

The gap between the part-time sides of the First Division and the full-time professionals of the Premiership is just too great. It appears that Ebbw Vale may be the last side to cross the divide successfully. Something needs to be done to help the emerging sides cross that gap, and central contracting is one development which could address this problem; Graham Henry is keen to introduce a central contracting system which would give the WRU greater control over players. The contract would stipulate the number of games a player could play per season; Graham has suggested that thirty games, including eight Tests, would be optimum. This, of course, could create conflict between the union and the leading clubs. Imagine a side which was pushing for the final qualifying place in Europe being told by the union that a leading player had played his quota of games, and had to be rested for a crunch fixture.

Another feature of central contracting would be that the union could place players with new clubs. This would ensure that younger players got more first-team football, but it would probably be opposed by the clubs. The bigger clubs have built up strong squads, which results in many players spending a disproportionate amount of time on the substitutes' bench. A good illustration of this is the position of Alix Popham of Newport. Popham is a promising number 8, but he is fighting for his place in the Newport team, where Gary Teichmann is the obvious first choice. Under central contracting, Popham could be moved to one of the weaker sides where he would get regular games.

Conflict between the union and the clubs could be easily resolved if both parties adopt a constructive attitude. This can be done, as is shown by Wasps' decision to allow Lawrence Dallaglio to miss the opening month of the season. The management at Wasps have taken the long-term view in resting Dallaglio. It will benefit the player if he is fresher when the next international season comes around, and will improve his chances of gaining a place on the Lions tour. What is good for England and the Lions is also good for the player and his club.

The European competitions have recently emerged as another force in improving standards within the domestic game. The European Cup and Shield have not enjoyed the easiest of births, but they are now firmly established and people are beginning to appreciate their worth. As yet the European Cup has not captured the imagination of the public in quite the same way as the Super 12 tournament has, but it is a great competition. Unfortunately its progress has been marred by events off the field, but on the field the European Cup has been a great success in rugby terms, and the players in Wales's top clubs relish the opportunity to pit themselves against the best sides in Europe. Initially it was predicted that the tournament would be dominated by the French and a few top English clubs, but Munster's victory, followed by that of the relatively unfashionable side Northampton, has done much to dispel that myth.

The European Shield is very much seen as the poor cousin of the more illustrious Heineken Cup. This is a rather unfair perception of the competition. There is undoubtedly strength in depth in both the English and French leagues, and this tournament offers a higher standard of competition than is available in the domestic league. The 2000–01 campaign will see sides such as Newcastle Falcons, Harlequins, Beziers and Brive competing against Welsh sides, proving just how competitive the tournament has become. As with the more prestigious tournament, it offers players the opportunity to experience different styles of play and stretches teams to the full.

In the longer term, a Celtic League is proposed for the

The Dragon Awakes

2001–02 season, and this should strengthen the competition. The Celtic League will consist of the four Irish districts, the two Scottish super-sides and eight Welsh teams, and will give an edge to the current season as teams compete to qualify for the league.

The Celtic League appears, on the face of it, to be a good idea. However, there are concerns about its structure: the Scottish district sides, Edinburgh Reivers and Glasgow Caledonians, have not really punched their weight in the Welsh–Scottish League. This may be because the two sides are guaranteed their places, both in the league and in the Heineken Cup – while the Welsh sides are fighting to avoid relegation or to win a place in the hugely remunerative European Cup, the Scots can freewheel. The question is, will this be the same for the four Irish district sides involved in the proposed Celtic League? If this is the case, it will lessen the urgency of the competition.

It seems somewhat unfair that Welsh clubs will be penalised by relegation without necessarily being the weakest side in the tournament. It is conceivable, under this scenario, that a Welsh side could come eighth in the league and still be relegated because the six teams below them are all Scottish and Irish, and therefore safeguarded against relegation.

It is important that the Celtic League is seen to be competitive and meaningful, so the unions must get sponsorship to give the league credibility. Sponsorship is also crucial in order to raise much needed revenue for cash-strapped clubs. Once again, money, or the lack of it, appears to be a major factor stopping Wales from competing on the world stage. We need a strong league to produce players of international calibre, and this can only be achieved if we have a significant number of well run, competitive clubs. At present most of the leading clubs are struggling to keep going. In recent seasons the WRU has bailed out Llanelli and Neath, both of whom got into financial difficulties. Ebbw Vale also had money problems, which caused them to disband what was becoming a very powerful side.

THE DRAGON AWAKES

The strong sides in Wales are those that have enjoyed huge investment from wealthy individuals: Peter Thomas at Cardiff, Tony Brown at Newport and Leighton Samuel at Bridgend have secured their clubs for the time being. Presumably even these people do not have bottomless pockets, and they will expect a return on their investment at some point. When the investors' money dries up, will these clubs be sustainable? I think not. The amount of money available to a Welsh club playing in the Welsh–Scottish League is approximately 30 per cent of that given to a side playing in England's Zurich Premiership. The lowest club in that league receives £1 million per season, compared to £300,000 per season for a top Welsh club.

Not surprisingly, Welsh clubs find it hard to compete in Europe when they are at such a huge economic disadvantage. The advantage of extra cash is not purely a matter of buying in better players. It is also about creating an environment conducive to the pursuit of excellence. It must be hard to stay focused on the job in hand when you are unsure about whether or not you will get paid next week. It must also have a demoralising effect on a squad to see key players being sold off in order to balance the books. Rugby union today is a business, and teams will not perform well if the business is run on a hand-to-mouth existence. In addition, the Welsh League will never be balanced when there is such financial disparity between the member clubs.

At the moment, it appears that you can buy success in the Welsh–Scottish League. It is proving hard for clubs to compete with the chequebooks at Newport and Cardiff, but while clubs rely on input from wealthy private individuals the game cannot be viewed as secure. Witness events at Newcastle Falcons: Sir John Hall's millions brought great players to the club and bought success. When he decided to remove that support the club was thrown into turmoil, from which it has yet to fully recover.

The plan for the Celtic League appears to be that it will run in addition to the Welsh–Scottish League. I fear that this may result in overkill, and that it could reduce the Welsh–Scottish League to a meaningless competition. If European Cup places are decided by positioning in the Celtic League, what is the purpose of the Welsh-Scottish League? It is being run partly to ensure that all the leading Welsh clubs get to play one another. This could be achieved by running the Celtic League as a simple league rather than organising it in two conferences. If there were to be fourteen teams in the new league it would mean twenty-six games per team, which should not be unmanageable for teams running squads of thirty players. In fact, players will take part in a similar number of matches if they are involved in both the Celtic and the Welsh–Scottish Leagues.

The Celtic League is definitely a good move, although obviously a competition including the English clubs would be preferable. However, it is crucial that the unions get the structure right from the start. There has been too much chopping and changing in the structure of the game in recent years. This lack of stability has alienated a lot of the support from the game, and this, as much as the form of the national side, has been a factor in the lack of support for matches at club level. What is needed now is a period of stability.

A British Cup is also projected for the 2000–01 season, and this could provide still more meaningful competition. The danger here is that, as with so many tournaments, players could be overplayed, sacrificed to the ambition of their clubs. Another opposing danger is that the cup may not be taken seriously. If the prize money is not substantial, or if a place in Europe is not attached to winning the cup, it will be treated as a tournament for second-string teams. This could be a good thing if viewed as an opportunity to run development teams, which would allow younger players an opportunity to play high-quality competitive rugby against strong opposition. However, I don't think this would have much appeal to spectators or to potential sponsors.

The Dragon Awakes

This season will also see the introduction, in Wales, of an Under-21 league, which should help in the development of the next generation of players and would make a British Cup superfluous as a development exercise. We seem to be coming dangerously close to overkill in the newly proposed structure. If all the plans come to fruition, in 2001 Welsh clubs could be playing in a Celtic League, the Welsh–Scottish League, the British Cup, the Welsh Cup, the Heineken Cup or European Shield, plus the Under-21 development league. Of these only two, the Celtic League which would decide places in Europe, and the European Cup, would have any meaning. This appears to me to be a blueprint for disaster. There would necessarily be a hierarchy amongst these tournaments, with clubs targeting the Celtic League and the European competitions. The others would become increasingly marginalised, and the fans would stay away in droves!

If this situation is allowed to develop, the Welsh clubs will be stuck with an unwieldy system which satisfies no one. We would be on the all-too-familiar merry-go-round. After a couple of seasons with the new system, we would have dissatisfaction and a call for change. The leading clubs would then start to lobby for a British League again. The English clubs, who have maintained all along that they are happy with the status quo, would be in a position of strength – any British League would only get off the ground if it had their full and unreserved backing. They might be prepared to accept a British League, provided none of the English Premiership sides lost out. I imagine they would suggest that Wales's input to the league should be four teams, probably Cardiff, Newport, Swansea and Llanelli, and we would be back to Graham Henry's original proposal for four super-clubs.

There are obvious merits in concentrating all our best players in a few clubs, but also real dangers. Firstly, it would be hugely divisive and would cause great disruption in the Welsh game. More importantly, we would be reducing our playing base to a ridiculously small number. With only four teams in Wales, the Welsh coach would, effectively, have 120 players from which to select his team. This number would be reduced significantly by the presence in these teams of foreign stars. At present, there are at least three or four foreign players in the leading Welsh teams – Newport already boast eight non-Welsh qualified players in their squad – and I would guess that this number would increase in the super-clubs. The competition in a British League would be intense, and club owners would invest in star players from abroad in order to compete.

It is not inconceivable that, in pursuit of honours, a Welsh club would take the same approach as Chelsea Football Club. Last season, Chelsea put out a side without a single English player in the team. If Newport or Cardiff were to adopt a similar tactic, the player base in Wales would be laughably low. This is definitely a worst-case scenario, but it is a possibility. The WRU would argue that they would include a clause requiring sides to field a certain number of Welsh-born players, but in practice this would be unenforceable. In fact, such a clause supposedly exists in the current rules of the Welsh–Scottish League, but Newport have ignored it without receiving any punishment. Given the ability of the unions to get it totally wrong, who would bet against them fouling up in just this manner? The structure of the game in Wales, and in Britain as a whole, needs to be looked at very carefully.

Ideally, we need a season structured to prepare players for international rugby. There should be a progressive structure, with the Celtic League matches being played in the first half of the season. This would decide qualification for the European competitions, which could be played after Christmas, with the Six Nations following on from that.

The Dragon Awakes

Ultimately, the strength of Welsh rugby is dependent on the strength of Northern Hemisphere rugby as a whole. It is no good for anyone in the Northern Hemisphere if the Six Nations tournament is totally dominated by England and France – those two teams need the challenge of tough international football on a regular basis, and they can only get that if Wales, Scotland, Ireland and eventually Italy are all strong. Australia, New Zealand and South Africa are the dominant forces in world rugby and they benefit tremendously from playing against one another in the Tri-Nations. Their strength, compared to the European nations, will increase if they are playing competitive internationals while the English or French are involved in training-style games against weak opposition. The ideal solution for all the Home Nations would be a British league, but Welsh involvement in this must be significant; we would need eight Welsh teams in the league, with relegation and promotion a possibility.

The involvement of the French in a European league would also be beneficial. The difficulty here lies, again, in the conflict between the needs of the national sides and the vested interests of the club owners. It seems likely that the leading clubs will want this to become a cartel, without relegation from and promotion to the new league, a situation which would be counter-productive by giving the teams at the bottom too much of a comfort zone.

I can still see the merit of having super-clubs, in the manner of the Super 12 teams, and I think the future for these super-teams lies in the European competitions. Perhaps one way forward would be to have three district sides representing Wales in Europe together with the Celtic League champions, or the highest-placed Welsh side in the League. So if Cardiff win the Celtic League or come second to an Irish or Scottish side, they would go into the European Cup along with sides representing East, West and Mid-Wales. The three district sides would draw on the leading players from the other Welsh clubs in the league and would rotate their home games around the grounds of the teams in the league, giving all supporters a chance to see games on their home ground.

Undoubtedly, we need a strong domestic or British league as a base for player development, but increasingly the European competition is going to dominate the game in Britain. Building a Welsh team that can compete consistently at the highest level, against New Zealand, Australia and South Africa, should be the ultimate aim of everybody in the game. This can only be achieved if a structure which satisfies the vested interests of the club owners, the needs of the players and desires of the supporters is put in place. In this sense, the future of Welsh rugby may be beyond the control of Graham Henry.

Graham Henry really has worked miracles in a relatively short time. Ultimately, he will be judged by Wales's performance in the 2003 World Cup. He has made a great start, but there remains much to be done. His next three years in charge promise to be just as interesting as the first two. He may have succeeded in waking up the slumbering dragon of Welsh rugby, but in the next three years he must make it breathe fire once again.

STATISTICS
WALES UNDER GRAHAM HENRY

14 NOVEMBER 1998 AT WEMBLEY STADIUM, LONDON
Wales 20 South Africa 28

WALES
S.P. Howarth
G. Thomas
M. Taylor
I.S. Gibbs
D.R. James
N.R. Jenkins
R. Howley
A.L.P. Lewis
J.M. Humphreys
C.T. Anthony
J.C. Quinnell
C.P. Wyatt
C.L. Charvis
L.S. Quinnell
M.E. Williams

SUBS
D.R. Morris
B.R. Evans

SOUTH AFRICA
P.C. Montgomery
C.S. Terblanche
A.H. Snyman
P.F. Smith
P. Rossouw
H.W. Honiball
J.H. van der Westhuizen
R.B. Kempson
J. Dalton
A.C. Garvey
M.G. Andrews
K. Otto
J. Erasmus
G.H. Teichmann
A.G. Venter

SUBS
A.H. 'Ollie' le Roux
R.B. Skinstad

The Dragon Awakes

SCORERS
Wales	T: Gareth Thomas
	P: Neil Jenkins 5

South Africa	T: Joost van der Westhuizen, Andre Venter, pen. try
	C: Franco Smith 2
	P: Franco Smith 3

21 NOVEMBER 1998 AT STRADEY PARK, LLANELLI
Wales 43 Argentina 30

WALES
S.P. Howarth
G. Thomas
M. Taylor
I.S. Gibbs
D.R. James
N.R. Jenkins
R. Howley
A.L.P. Lewis
J.M. Humphreys
C.T. Anthony
J.C. Quinnell
C.P. Wyatt
C.L. Charvis
L.S. Quinnell
M.E. Williams

ARGENTINA
M. Contepomi
I. Corletto
J. Orengo
L. Arbizu
F. Soler
F. Contepomi
A. Pichot
M. Reggiardo
F.E. Mendez
O. Hasan-Jalil
P.L. Sporleder
A. Allub
M. Durand
P.J. Camerlinckx
M.A. Ruiz

SUBS
M.J. Voyle
B.H. Williams

SUBS
E. Simone
D.L. Albanese
M. Ledesma
R.A. Martin

SCORERS
Wales	T: Colin Charvis 2, Dafydd James, Mark Taylor
	C: Neil Jenkins 4
	P: Neil Jenkins 5

The Dragon Awakes

Argentina   T: Agustin Pichot, Luis Sporleder, Felipe Contepomi, pen. try
C: Felipe Contepomi 2
P: Felipe Contepomi 2

6 FEBRUARY 1999 AT MURRAYFIELD, EDINBURGH
Scotland 33 Wales 20

SCOTLAND
G.H. Metcalfe
C.A. Murray
G.P.J. Townsend
J.A. Leslie
K.M. Logan
D.W. Hodge
G. Armstrong
T.J. Smith
G.C. Bulloch
A.P. Burnell
S. Murray
G.W. Weir
P. Walton
E.W. Peters
M.D. Leslie

SUBS
A.V. Tait
A.C. Pountney
S.B. Grimes
D.I.W. Hilton

WALES
S.P. Howarth
M.F.D. Robinson
A.G. Bateman
I.S. Gibbs
D.R. James
N.R. Jenkins
R. Howley
D.R. Morris
J.M. Humphreys
C.T. Anthony
I. Gough
C.P. Wyatt
C.L. Charvis
L.S. Quinnell
M.E. Williams

SUBS
B. Williams
M.J. Voyle

SCORERS
Scotland   T: John Leslie, Gregor Townsend, Alan Tait, Scott Murray
C: Kenny Logan 2
P: Kenny Logan 2, Duncan Hodge

The Dragon Awakes

Wales   T: Dafydd James, Scott Gibbs
               C: Neil Jenkins 2
               P: Neil Jenkins 2

20 FEBRUARY 1999 AT WEMBLEY STADIUM, LONDON
Wales 23 Ireland 29

WALES	**IRELAND**
S.P. Howarth	C.M.P. O'Shea
M.F.D. Robinson	J.P. Bishop
M. Taylor	K.M. Maggs
I.S. Gibbs	J.C. Bell
D.R. James	N.K.P.J. Woods
N.R. Jenkins	D.G. Humphreys
R. Howley	C.D. McGuinness
D.R. Morris	P.S. Wallace
B.R. Williams	K.G.M. Wood
D. Young	P.M.N. Clohessy
J.C. Quinnell	P.S. Johns
C.P. Wyatt	J.W. Davidson
C.L. Charvis	D. O'Cuinneagain
L.S. Quinnell	E.R.P. Miller
M.E. Williams	A.J. Ward

SUBS	**SUBS**
G.R. Jenkins	J.M. Fitzpatrick
C.T. Anthony	M.J. Galwey
M.J. Voyle	V.C.P. Costello

SCORERS

Wales   T: Craig Quinnell, Shane Howarth
            C: Neil Jenkins 2
            P: Neil Jenkins 3

Ireland   T: Kevin Maggs, Keith Wood
            C: David Humphreys 2
            P: David Humphreys 3
           DG: David Humphreys 2

6 MARCH 1999 AT STADE DE FRANCE, PARIS
France 33 Wales 34

FRANCE
E. Ntamack
P. Bernat-Salles
R. Dourthe
F. Comba
T. Lombard
T. Castaignède
P. Carbonneau
C. Califano
R. Ibanez
F. Tournaire
O. Brouzet
F. Pelous
P. Benetton
T. Lièvremont
M. Raynaud

SUBS
D. Aucagne
X. Garbajosa
S. Marconnet
R. Castel

WALES
S.P. Howarth
M.F.D. Robinson
M. Taylor
I.S. Gibbs
D.R. James
N.R. Jenkins
R. Howley
P.J.D. Rogers
G.R. Jenkins
B.R. Evans
J.C. Quinnell
C.P. Wyatt
C.L. Charvis
L.S. Quinnell
B.D. Sinkinson

SUBS
G. Thomas
D.S. Llewellyn
A.L.P. Lewis

SCORERS
France   T: Emile Ntamack 3, Thomas Castaignède
                C: Thomas Castaignède 2
                P: Thomas Castaignède 3

Wales   T: Colin Charvis, Craig Quinnell, Dafydd James
                C: Neil Jenkins 2
                P: Neil Jenkins 5

20 MARCH 1999 AT STADIO COMMUNALE DI MONIGO, TREVISO
Italy 21 Wales 60

ITALY	**WALES**
J.-A. Pertile	S.P. Howarth
F. Roselli	G. Thomas
A.C. Stoica	M. Taylor
L. Martin	I.S. Gibbs
D. Dallan	D.R. James
D. Dominguez	N.R. Jenkins
A. Troncon	R. Howley
M. Cuttitta	P.J.D. Rogers
A. Moscardi	G.R. Jenkins
F. Properzi-Curti	B.R. Evans
W. Cristofoletto	J.C. Quinnell
M. Giacheri	C.P. Wyatt
M. Giovanelli	C.L. Charvis
D. Scaglia	L.S. Quinnell
A. Sgorlon	B.D. Sinkinson

SUBS	**SUBS**
M. Baroni	N.J. Walne
A. Castellani	N. Boobyer
S. Stocco	D.S. Llewellyn
S. Saviozzi	B.R. Williams
	M.J. Voyle
	G. Lewis
	D.R. Morris

SCORERS

Italy   T: Luca Martin, Diego Scaglia
C: Diego Dominguez
P: Diego Dominguez 3

Wales   T: Gareth Thomas 4, Craig Quinnell, Neil Jenkins, Rob Howley
C: Neil Jenkins 5
P: Neil Jenkins 5

11 APRIL 1999 AT WEMBLEY STADIUM, LONDON
Wales 32 England 31

WALES	**ENGLAND**
S.P. Howarth	M.B. Perry
G. Thomas	D. Luger
M. Taylor	J.P. Wilkinson
I.S. Gibbs	B.J. Mather
D.R. James	S.M. Hanley
N.R. Jenkins	M.J. Catt
R. Howley	M.J.S. Dawson
P.J.D. Rogers	J. Leonard
G.R. Jenkins	R. Cockerill
B.R. Evans	D.J. Garforth
J.C. Quinnell	M.O. Johnson
C.P. Wyatt	T.A.K. Rodber
C.L. Charvis	R.A. Hill
L.S. Quinnell	L.B.N. Dallaglio
B.D. Sinkinson	N.A. Back

SUBS
N.J. Walne
A.L.P. Lewis
D. Young

SUB
V.E. Ubogu

SCORERS

Wales   T: Shane Howarth, Scott Gibbs
              C: Neil Jenkins 2
              P: Neil Jenkins 6

England   T: Dan Luger, Steve Hanley, Richard Hill
              C: Jonny Wilkinson 2
              P: Jonny Wilkinson 4

5 JUNE 1999 AT CARRIL OESTE STADIUM, BUENOS AIRES
Argentina 26 Wales 36

ARGENTINA
D.L. Albanese
O. Bartolucci
E. Simone
L. Arbizu
E. Jurado
G. Quesada
A. Pichot
R. Grau
F.E. Mendez
M. Reggiardo
P.L. Sporleder
A. Allub
I.F. Lobbe
P.J. Camerlinckx
R.A. Martin

WALES
S.P. Howarth
M.F.D. Robinson
M. Taylor
A.G. Bateman
D.R. James
N.R. Jenkins
R. Howley
P.J.D. Rogers
G.R. Jenkins
B.R. Evans
J.C. Quinnell
C.P. Wyatt
C.L. Charvis
L.S. Quinnell
B.D. Sinkinson

SUBS
O. Hasan-Jalil
G. Longo
L. Ostiglia

SUBS
A.L.P. Lewis
D. Young

SCORERS
Argentina   T: Gonzalo Quesada, Octavio Bartolucci
C: Gonzalo Quesada 2
P: Gonzalo Quesada 4

Wales   T: Dafydd James, Brett Sinkinson, Chris Wyatt
C: Neil Jenkins 3
P: Neil Jenkins 4
DG: Shane Howarth

12 JUNE 1999 AT CARRIL OESTE STADIUM, BUENOS AIRES
Argentina 16 Wales 23

ARGENTINA
D.L. Albanese
O. Bartolucci
J. Orengo
L. Arbizu
G.F. Camardon
F. Contepomi
A. Pichot
R. Grau
F.E. Mendez
M. Reggiardo
P.L. Sporleder
I.F. Lobbe
R.A. Martin
G. Longo
M.A. Ruiz

SUBS
J. Cilley
A. Allub
M. Ledesma
L. Ostiglia
O. Hasan-Jalil

WALES
S.P. Howarth
G. Thomas
M. Taylor
A.G. Bateman
D.R. James
N.R. Jenkins
R. Howley
P.J.D. Rogers
G.R. Jenkins
B.R. Evans
J.C. Quinnell
C.P. Wyatt
G. Lewis
L.S. Quinnell
B.D. Sinkinson

SUBS
D. Young
J.M. Humphreys
A.L.P. Lewis

SCORERS
Argentina   T: José Orengo
                C: José Cilley
                P: Felipe Contepomi 3

Wales   T: Garin Jenkins
                P: Neil Jenkins 5
                DG: Neil Jenkins

26 JUNE 1999 AT THE MILLENNIUM STADIUM, CARDIFF
Wales 29 South Africa 19

WALES
S.P. Howarth
G. Thomas
M. Taylor
A.G. Bateman
D.R. James
N.R. Jenkins
R. Howley
P.J.D. Rogers
G.R. Jenkins
D. Young
J.C. Quinnell
C.P. Wyatt
C.L. Charvis
L.S. Quinnell
B.D. Sinkinson

SUBS
A.L.P. Lewis
J.M. Humphreys
M.J. Voyle

SOUTH AFRICA
P.C. Montgomery
C.S. Terblanche
P.G. Muller
J.C. Mulder
P. Rossouw
A.J.C. van Straaten
W. Swanepoel
R.B. Kempson
A.E. Drotske
I.J. Visagie
C.S. Boome
K. Otto
C.P.J. Krige
G.H. Teichmann
J. Erasmus

SUBS
G.S. du Toit
D.J.B. Von Hoesslin
A.H. le Roux
A.G. Venter

SCORERS
Wales T: Mark Taylor, Gareth Thomas
C: Neil Jenkins 2
P: Neil Jenkins 5

South Africa T: Werner Swanepoel, Percy Montgomery
P: Braam van Straaten 2, Gaffie du Toit

21 AUGUST 1999 AT THE MILLENNIUM STADIUM, CARDIFF
Wales 33 Canada 19

WALES	**CANADA**
S.P. Howarth	D.S. Stewart
N.J. Walne	W. Stanley
L.B. Davies	D.C. Lougheed
I.S. Gibbs	S. Bryan
A.G. Bateman	C. Smith
N.R. Jenkins	G.L. Rees
R. Howley	M.E. Williams
P.J.D. Rogers	R. Snow
J.M. Humphreys	M.E. Cardinal
B.R. Evans	R. Bice
J.C. Quinnell	J.N. Tait
A.S. Moore	M.B. James
G. Lewis	J.R. Hutchinson
L.S. Quinnell	A.J. Charron
M.E. Williams	D.R. Baugh

SUBS	**SUBS**
S. Jones	R.P. Ross
A.L.P. Lewis	J. Thiel
D. Young	M. Schmid
G.O. Llewellyn	R. Banks
C.P. Wyatt	

SCORERS
Wales   T: Neil Jenkins, Nick Walne
               C: Neil Jenkins
               P: Neil Jenkins 7

Canada   T: Dave Lougheed
               C: Gareth Rees
               P: Gareth Rees 3
               DG: Gareth Rees

28 AUGUST 1999 AT THE MILLENNIUM STADIUM, CARDIFF
Wales 34 France 23

WALES	**FRANCE**
S.P. Howarth	U. Mola
G. Thomas	X. Garbajosa
M. Taylor	R. Dourthe
I.S. Gibbs	S. Glas
D.R. James	C. Dominici
N.R. Jenkins	T. Castaignède
R. Howley	S. Castaignède
P.J.D. Rogers	C. Califano
G.R. Jenkins	R. Ibanez
D. Young	P.S. de Villiers
J.C. Quinnell	A. Benazzi
C.P. Wyatt	F. Pelous
C.L. Charvis	M. Lièvremont
L.S. Quinnell	T. Lièvremont
B.D. Sinkinson	O. Magne

SUB	**SUBS**
M.J. Voyle	E. Ntamack
	D. Auradou
	C. Lamaison
	P. Mignoni
	M. Dal Maso
	C. Soulette
	L. Mallier

SCORERS
Wales   T: Dafydd James
           C: Neil Jenkins
           P: Neil Jenkins 9

France   T: Lionel Mallier, Pierre Mignoni
           C: Richard Dourthe, Christophe Lamaison
           P: Richard Dourthe 2, Christophe Lamaison

30 AUGUST 1999 AT THE MILLENNIUM STADIUM, CARDIFF
Wales 53 USA 24 (not full international)

WALES	**USA**
N. Boobyer	K. Shuman
N.J. Walne	V. Anitoni
A. Marinos	J. Grobler
L.B. Davies	T. Takau
A.G. Bateman	B. Hightower
S. Jones	M. Williams
D.S. Llewellyn	K. Dalzell
A.L.P. Lewis	G. Sucher
J.M. Humphreys	T. Billups
B.R. Evans	R. Lehner
G.O. Llewellyn	L. Gross
M.J. Voyle	A. Parker
G. Lewis	D. Hodges
H. Jenkins	D. Lyle
M.E. Williams	R. Lumkong

THE RUGBY WORLD CUP

1 OCTOBER 1999 AT THE MILLENNIUM STADIUM, CARDIFF
Wales 23 Argentina 18

WALES	**ARGENTINA**
S.P. Howarth	M. Contepomi
G. Thomas	O. Bartolucci
M. Taylor	E. Simone
I.S. Gibbs	L. Arbizu
D.R. James	D.L. Albanese
N.R. Jenkins	G. Quesada
R. Howley	A. Pichot
P.J.D. Rogers	R. Grau
G.R. Jenkins	M. Ledesma
D. Young	M. Reggiardo
J.C. Quinnell	I.F. Lobbe

C.P. Wyatt
C.L. Charvis
L.S. Quinnell
B.D. Sinkinson

A. Allub
S. Phelan
G. Longo
L. Ostiglia

SUB
J. Jones-Hughes

SUBS
G.F. Camardon
O. Hasan-Jalil
R.A. Martin

SCORERS
Wales   T: Colin Charvis, Mark Taylor
           C: Neil Jenkins 2
           P: Neil Jenkins 3

Argentina P: Gonzalo Quesada 6

9 OCTOBER 1999 AT THE MILLENNIUM STADIUM, CARDIFF
Wales 64 Japan 15

WALES
S.P. Howarth
J. Jones-Hughes
M. Taylor
I.S. Gibbs
A.G. Bateman
N.R. Jenkins
R. Howley
P.J.D. Rogers
G.R. Jenkins
D. Young
J.C. Quinnell
M.J. Voyle
M.E. Williams
G. Lewis
B.D. Sinkinson

JAPAN
T. Hirao
D. Ohata
Y. Motoki
A. McCormick
P. Tuidraki
K. Hirose
G. Bachop
S. Hasegawa
M. Kunda
N. Nakamura
R. Gordon
H. Tanuma
N. Okubo
J. Joseph
G. Smith

THE DRAGON AWAKES

SUBS
G. Thomas
D.S. Llewellyn
A.L.P. Lewis
J.M. Humphreys
B.R. Evans
C.P. Wyatt

SUBS
W. Murata
T. Nakamichi
M. Sakata
Y. Sakuraba
T. Ito

SCORERS
Wales   T: Mark Taylor 2, Gareth Thomas, Rob Howley, Scott Gibbs, Shane Howarth, David Llewellyn, Allan Bateman, pen. try
C: Neil Jenkins 8
P: Neil Jenkins

Japan   T: Daisuke Ohata, Patiliai Tuidraki
C: Keiji Hirose
P: Keiji Hirose

14 OCTOBER 1999 AT THE MILLENNIUM STADIUM, CARDIFF
Wales 31 Samoa 38

WALES
S.P. Howarth
G. Thomas
M. Taylor
I.S. Gibbs
D.R. James
N.R. Jenkins
R. Howley
P.J.D. Rogers
G.R. Jenkins
D. Young
G.O. Llewellyn
C.P. Wyatt
M.E. Williams
J.C. Quinnell
B.D. Sinkinson

SAMOA
S. Leaega
B. Lima
G. Leaupepe
T. Vaega
V. Tuigamala
S.J. Bachop
S. So'oialo
B. Reidy
T. Leota
R. Ale
L. Tone
L. Faniko
P.J. Paramore
P.R. Lam
C. Glendinning

THE DRAGON AWAKES

SUBS
A.L.P. Lewis
B.R. Evans

SUBS
T.L. Fanolua
E. Va'a
O. Mataulau
M. Mika
S. Ta'ala
S. Sititi

SCORERS
Wales   T: Gareth Thomas 2, pen. try
           C: Neil Jenkins 2
           P: Neil Jenkins 4

Samoa   T: Stephen Bachop 2, Pat Lam, Silao Leaega, Lio Falaniko
            C: Silao Leaega 5
            P: Silao Leaega

23 OCTOBER 1999 AT THE MILLENNIUM STADIUM, CARDIFF
Wales 9 Australia 24

WALES
S.P. Howarth
G. Thomas
M. Taylor
I.S. Gibbs
D.R. James
N.R. Jenkins
R. Howley
P.J.D. Rogers
G.R. Jenkins
D. Young
J.C. Quinnell
C.P. Wyatt
C.L. Charvis
L.S. Quinnell
B.D. Sinkinson

AUSTRALIA
M.C. Burke
B.N. Tune
D.J. Herbert
T.J. Horan
J.W.C. Roff
S.J. Larkham
G.M. Gregan
R.L.L. Harry
M.A. Foley
A.T. Blades
D. Giffin
J.A. Eales
M.J. Cockbain
C.P. Strauss
D.J. Wilson

THE DRAGON AWAKES

SUBS
A.G. Bateman
A.L.P. Lewis
B.R. Evans
M.J. Voyle

SUBS
J.S. Little
J.A. Paul
M. Connors
O.D.A. Finegan

SCORERS
Wales   P: Neil Jenkins 3

Australia T: George Gregan 2, Ben Tune
           C: Matt Burke 3
           P: Matt Burke

SIX NATIONS CHAMPIONSHIP

5 FEBRUARY 2000 AT THE MILLENNIUM STADIUM, CARDIFF
Wales 3 France 36

WALES
S.P. Howarth
G. Thomas
M. Taylor
J. Jones-Hughes
D.R. James
N.R. Jenkins
R. Howley
P.J.D. Rogers
G.R. Jenkins
D. Young
I. Gough
C.P. Wyatt
C.L. Charvis
L.S. Quinnell
B.D. Sinkinson

FRANCE
T. Castaignède
E. Ntamack
R. Dourthe
T. Lombard
C. Dominici
C. Lamaison
F. Galthié
C. Califano
M. Dal Maso
F. Tournaire
O. Brouzet
L. Matiu
A. Benazzi
F. Pelous
O. Magne

The Dragon Awakes

SUBS
G. Lewis
M.J. Voyle
S.C. John
S. Williams
R. Smith
B.H. Williams

SUBS
D. Venditti
T. Lièvremont
R. Ibanez
P.S. de Villiers
S. Betson
C. Laussucq
A. Penaud

SCORERS
Wales   P: Neil Jenkins

France   T: Olivier Magne, Thomas Castaignède,
         Emile Ntamack
         C: Christophe Lamaison 3
         P: Christophe Lamaison 4
         DG: Christophe Lamaison

19 FEBRUARY 2000 AT THE MILLENNIUM STADIUM, CARDIFF
Wales 47 Italy 16

WALES
S.P. Howarth
G. Thomas
M. Taylor
A.G. Bateman
S. Williams
N.R. Jenkins
R. Howley
P.J.D. Rogers
G.R. Jenkins
D. Young
J.C. Quinnell
C.P. Wyatt
G. Lewis
L.S. Quinnell
B.D. Sinkinson

ITALY
M. Pini
A.C. Stoica
L. Martin
M. Rivaro
D. Dallan
D. Dominguez
A. Troncon
M. Cuttitta
A. Moscardi
T. Paoletti
G. Lanzi
A. Gritti
C. Checchinato
M. Bergamasco
W. Visser

SUBS
C.L. Charvis
B.H. Williams
I. Gough
S. Jones
D.R. James
S.C. John

SUBS
C. Orlandi
J. Francesio
A. Persico

SCORERS
Wales   T: Scott Quinnell, Shane Williams, Allan Bateman, Shane Howarth
C: Neil Jenkins 3
P: Neil Jenkins 7

Italy   T: Wilhelmus Visser
C: Diego Dominguez
P: Diego Dominguez 2
DG: Diego Dominguez

4 FEBRUARY 2000 AT TWICKENHAM, LONDON
England 46 Wales 12

ENGLAND
M.B. Perry
A.S. Healey
M. Tindall
M.J. Catt
B. Cohen
J.P. Wilkinson
M.J.S. Dawson
J. Leonard
P. Greening
P. Vickery
G. Archer
S. Shaw
R.A. Hill
L.B.N. Dallaglio
N.A. Back

WALES
S.P. Howarth
G. Thomas
M. Taylor
A.G. Bateman
S. Williams
N.R. Jenkins
R. Howley
P.J.D. Rogers
G.R. Jenkins
D. Young
J.C. Quinnell
C.P. Wyatt
C.L. Charvis
L.S. Quinnell
B.D. Sinkinson

The Dragon Awakes

SUB
M. Corry

SUBS
S. John
B.H. Williams
I. Gough
M.E. Williams

SCORERS
England   T: Phil Greening, Neil Back, Richard Hill, Lawrence Dallaglio, Ben Cohen
C: Jonny Wilkinson 3
P: Jonny Wilkinson 5

Wales   P: Neil Jenkins 3
DG: Neil Jenkins

18 MARCH 2000 AT THE MILLENNIUM STADIUM, CARDIFF
Wales 26 Scotland 18

WALES
M. Cardey
G. Thomas
M. Taylor
A.G. Bateman
S. Williams
S. Jones
R.H.StJ.B. Moon
P.J.D. Rogers
G.R. Jenkins
D. Young
I. Gough
A.S. Moore
N. Budgett
G. Lewis
C.L. Charvis

SCOTLAND
C. Paterson
C. Moir
G.P.J. Townsend
J.A. Leslie
G.H. Metcalfe
D.W. Hodge
A.D. Nicol
T.J. Smith
S. Brotherstone
M. Stewart
S. Murray
S.B. Grimes
M.D. Leslie
S. Reid
A.C. Pountney

SUBS
G.C. Bulloch
D.I.W. Hilton

188

The Dragon Awakes

SCORERS
Wales   T: Shane Williams 2
           C: Stephen Jones 2
           P: Stephen Jones 4

Scotland   T: Martin Leslie, Gregor Townsend
           C: Duncan Hodge
           P: Duncan Hodge 2

1 APRIL 2000 AT LANSDOWNE ROAD, DUBLIN
Ireland 19 Wales 23

IRELAND   **WALES**
G. Dempsey   R. Williams
S. Horgan   G. Thomas
B. O'Driscoll   A.G. Bateman
R. Henderson   I.S. Gibbs
D. Hickie   S. Williams
R. O'Gara   S. Jones
P. Stringer   R.H.StJ.B. Moon
P.M.N. Clohessy   P.J.D. Rogers
K.G.M. Wood   G.R. Jenkins
J. Hayes   D. Young
M.J. Galwey   I. Gough
M. O'Kelly   A.S. Moore
S. Easterby   N. Budgett
A. Foley   G. Lewis
K. Dawson   C.L. Charvis

SUBS   **SUBS**
J.W. Davidson   N.R. Jenkins
A.J. Ward   R. McBryde
D.G. Humphreys   D.R. James

SCORERS
Ireland   T: Shane Horgan
           C: Ronan O'Gara
           P: Ronan O'Gara 4

THE DRAGON AWAKES

Wales   T: Nathan Budgett, Stephen Jones
         C: Stephen Jones 2
         P: Stephen Jones, Neil Jenkins 2

WALES'S PLAYING RECORD UNDER GRAHAM HENRY

	P	W	L	D	FOR	AGAINST
Wales	21	14	7	0	625	538

Does not include USA game, for which caps were not awarded

PLAYERS USED BY GRAHAM HENRY

PLAYER	CAPS	TRIES	CONS	PENS	DGS	PTS
Backs						
Shane Howarth	19	4	0	0	1	23
Matt Cardey	1	0	0	0	0	0
Rhys Williams	1	0	0	0	0	0
Gareth Thomas	17	9	0	0	0	45
Mark Taylor	18	5	0	0	0	25
Scott Gibbs	14	3	0	0	0	15
Allan Bateman	11	2	0	0	0	10
Dafydd James	17	5	0	0	0	25
Jason Jones-Hughes	3	0	0	0	0	0
Leigh Davies	1	0	0	0	0	0
Neil Boobyer	1	0	0	0	0	0
Nick Walne	3	1	0	0	0	5
Shane Williams	5	3	0	0	0	15
Matthew Robinson	3	0	0	0	0	0
Neil Jenkins	20	2	39	85	2	349
Stephen Jones	4	1	4	5	0	28
Rob Howley	19	2	0	0	0	10
David Llewellyn	3	1	0	0	0	5
Richard Smith	1	0	0	0	0	0
Rupert Moon	2	0	0	0	0	0

The Dragon Awakes

Forwards

Andrew Lewis	11	0	0	0	0	0
Darren Morris	4	0	0	0	0	0
Peter Rogers	17	0	0	0	0	0
Spencer John	3	0	0	0	0	0
Chris Anthony	4	0	0	0	0	0
Ben Evans	10	0	0	0	0	0
David Young	16	0	0	0	0	0
Jonathan Humphreys	7	0	0	0	0	0
Garin Jenkins	17	1	0	0	0	5
Barry Williams	7	0	0	0	0	0
Robyn McBryde	1	0	0	0	0	0
Craig Quinnell	16	3	0	0	0	15
Chris Wyatt	19	1	0	0	0	5
Ian Gough	6	0	0	0	0	0
Mike Voyle	9	0	0	0	0	0
Andy Moore	3	0	0	0	0	0
Gareth Llewellyn	2	0	0	0	0	0
Colin Charvis	17	4	0	0	0	20
Geraint Lewis	8	0	0	0	0	0
Martyn Williams	8	0	0	0	0	0
Brett Sinkinson	14	1	0	0	0	5
Nathan Budgett	2	1	0	0	0	5
Scott Quinnell	18	1	0	0	0	5
Totals		50	43	90	3	615

Two penalty tries were awarded, totalling 10 points
Total points scored 625